EASY GUITAR WITH NOTES & TAB

The Very Best of GRATEFUL DEAD

ISBN 978-1-4950-0699-9

HAL•LEONARD® CORPORATION

7777 W. BLUEMOUND RD. P.O. BOX 13819 MILWAUKEE, WI 53213

Visit Hal Leonard Online at
www.halleonard.com

STRUM AND PICK PATTERNS

This chart contains the suggested strum and pick patterns that are referred to by number at the beginning of each song in this book. The symbols ⊓ and ∨ in the strum patterns refer to down and up strokes, respectively. The letters in the pick patterns indicate which right-hand fingers play which strings.

p = thumb
i = index finger
m = middle finger
a = ring finger

For example; Pick Pattern 2
is played: thumb - index - middle - ring

Strum Patterns   ## Pick Patterns

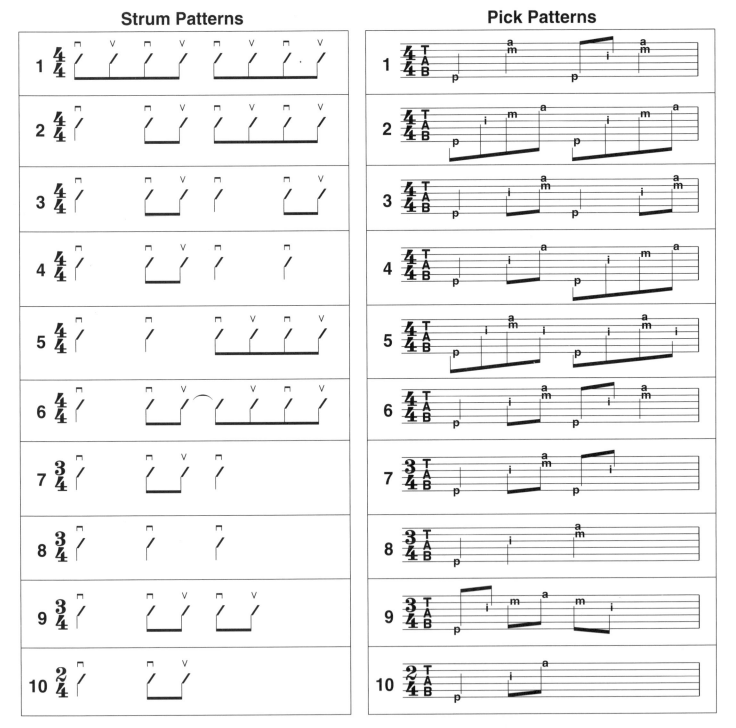

You can use the 3/4 Strum and Pick Patterns in songs written in compound meter (6/8, 9/8, 12/8, etc.). For example, you can accompany a song in 6/8 by playing the 3/4 pattern twice in each measure. The 4/4 Strum and Pick Patterns can be used for songs written in cut time (¢) by doubling the note time values in the patterns. Each pattern would therefore last two measures in cut time.

Truckin'

Words and Music by Jerry Garcia, Robert Hunter, Phil Lesh and Bob Weir

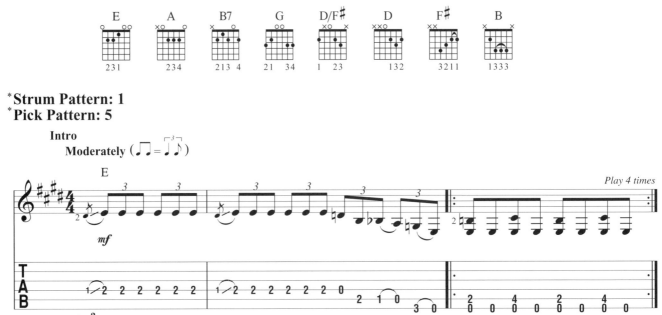

*Strum Pattern: 1
*Pick Pattern: 5

*Use Pattern 10 for 2/4 meas.

Chorus

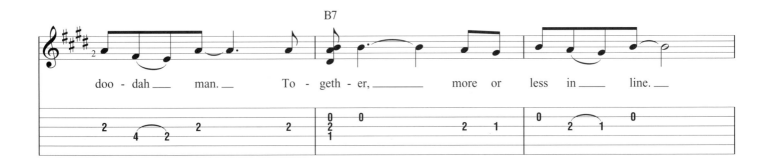

1. Truck - in', _____ got my chips cashed _ in, _____ keep truck - in', _____ like the

doo - dah ___ man. ___ To - geth - er, _____ more or less in ___ line. ___

Just keep truck - in' on. _____

%. Verse

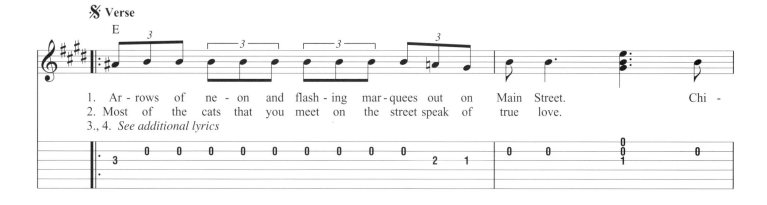

1. Ar - rows of ne - on and flash - ing mar - quees out on Main Street. Chi -
2. Most of the cats that you meet on the street speak of true love.
3., 4. *See additional lyrics*

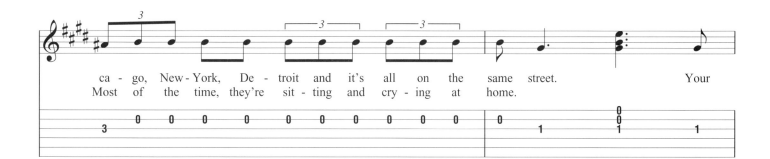

ca - go, New - York, De - troit and it's all on the same street. Your
Most of the time, they're sit - ting and cry - ing at home.

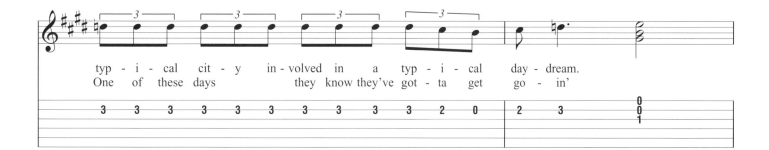

typ - i - cal cit - y in - volved in a typ - i - cal day - dream.
One of these days they know they've got - ta get go - in'

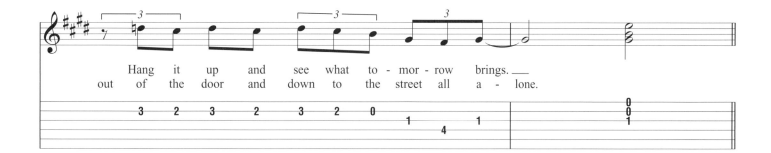

Hang it up and see what to - mor - row brings. ___
out of the door and down to the street all a - lone.

Chorus

2. Dal - las _____ got a soft ma - chine, Hous - ton, _____ too close to
3. Truck - in' _____ like the doo - dah ___ man, ___ once told me you got to
4., 5. *See additional lyrics*

long _____ strange trip it's been. _____

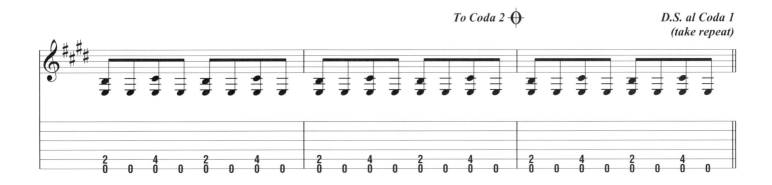

To Coda 2 ⊕　　　　　　　　　　　　　　　*D.S. al Coda 1*
(take repeat)

⊕ **Coda 1**　　　　　　　　　　**Verse**

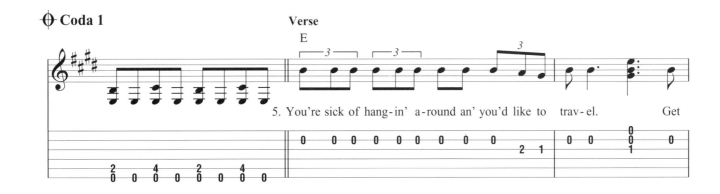

5. You're sick of hang-in' a-round an' you'd like to trav-el.　Get

tired of trav-el-in', you want to set-tle down. ＿　　I　guess they can't re-voke your soul for

D.S.S. al Coda 2

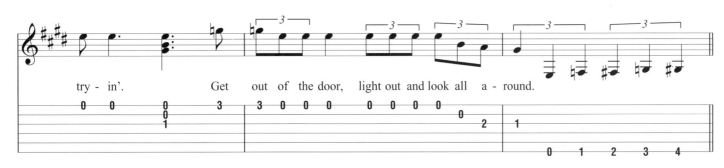

try-in'.　　Get　out　of　the door,　light out and look all　a-round.

Coda 2 Chorus

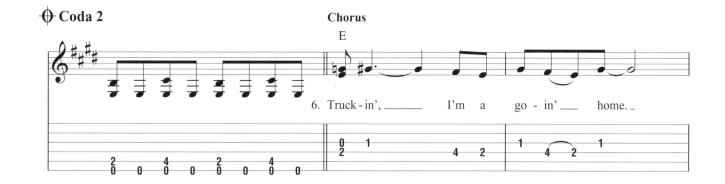

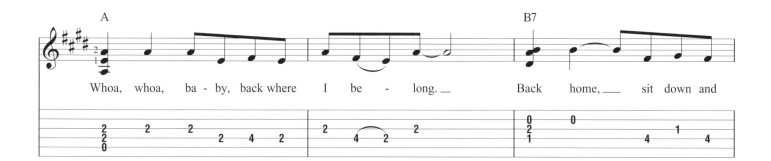

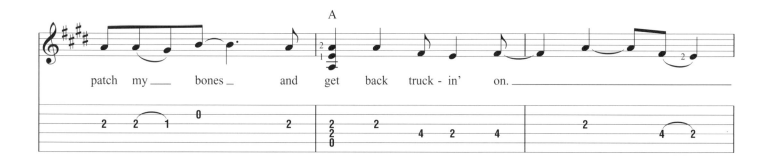

Outro-Guitar Solo *Repeat and fade*

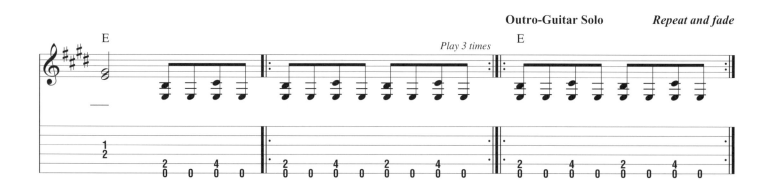

Additional Lyrics

3. What in the world ever became of Sweet Jane?
   She lost her sparkle, you know she isn't the same.
   Livin' on Reds, Vitamin C and cocaine,
   All a friend can say is ain't it a shame.

Chorus 4 Truckin' up to Buffalo,
   Been thinkin' you got to mellow slow.
   Takes time to pick a place to go,
   And just keep truckin' on.

4. Sittin' and starin' out of the hotel window,
   Got a tip they're gonna kick the door in again.
   I'd like to get some sleep before I travel,
   But if you got a warrant I guess you're gonna come in.

Chorus 5 Busted down on Bourbon Street,
   Set up like a bowlin' pin.
   Knocked down, it gets to wearing thin,
   They just won't let you be.

Sugar Magnolia

Words and Music by Bob Weir and Robert Hunter

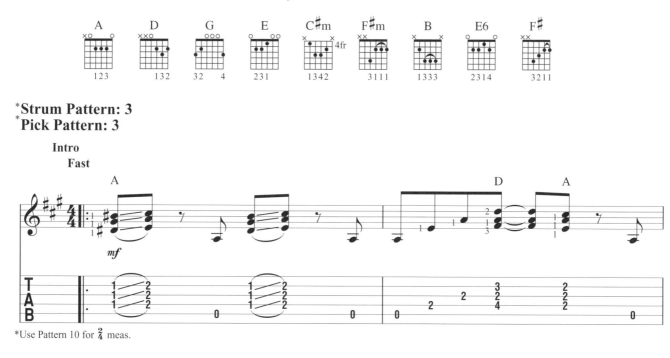

A   D   G   E   C#m   F#m   B   E6   F#

*Strum Pattern: 3
*Pick Pattern: 3

Intro

Fast

*Use Pattern 10 for 2/4 meas.

Verse

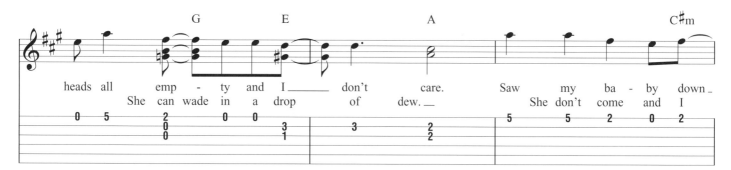

1. Sug - ar Mag - no - lia,   blos - soms bloom - ing,
3. Well, she come skim - min' through rays _____ of vio - let.

heads all emp - ty and I _____ don't care.   Saw my ba - by down ___
She can wade in a drop of dew. ___   She don't come and I

Verse

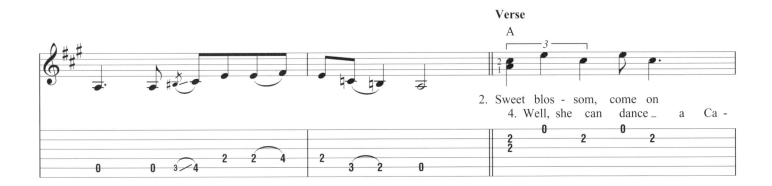

2. Sweet blos - som, come on
4. Well, she can dance _ a Ca -

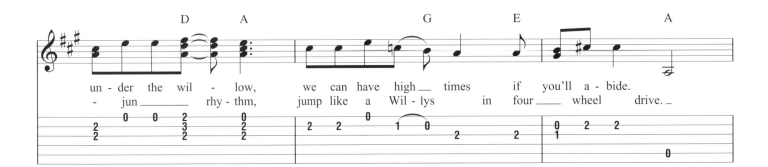

un - der the wil - low, we can have high _ times if you'll a - bide.
- jun _ rhy - thm, jump like a Wil - lys in four _ wheel drive.

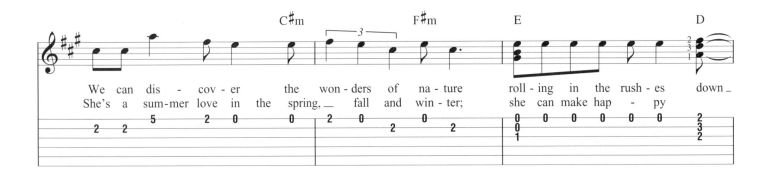

We can dis - cov - er the won - ders of na - ture roll - ing in the rush - es down _
She's a sum - mer love in the spring, _ fall and win - ter; she can make hap - py

To Coda 1 𝄌

_ by the riv - er - side.
an - y man a - live. _

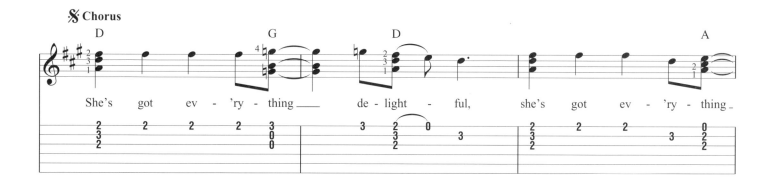

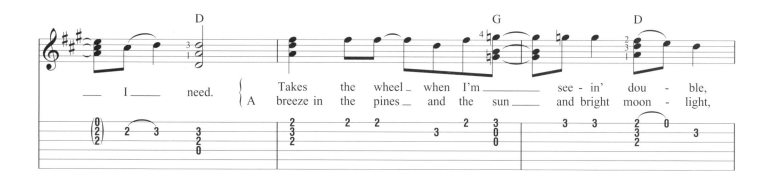

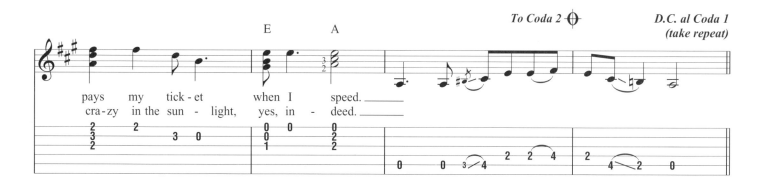

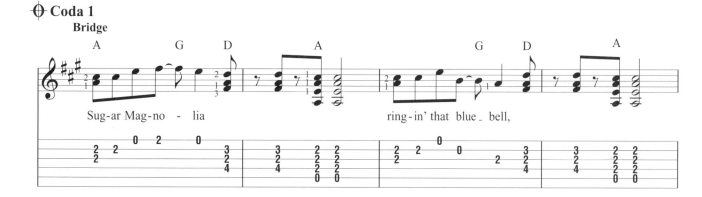

⊕ Coda 1

Bridge

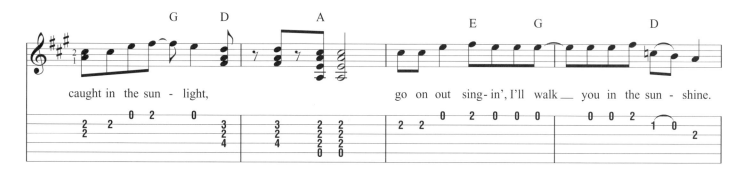

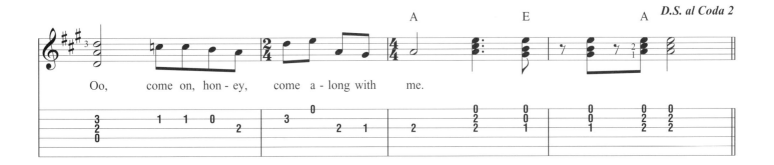

Oo, come on, hon-ey, come a-long with me.

⊕ Coda 2

Verse

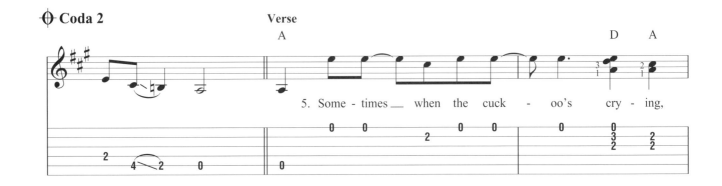

5. Some - times ___ when the cuck - oo's cry - ing,

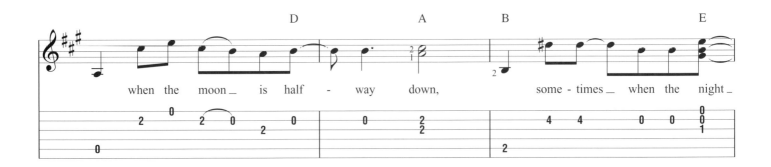

when the moon ___ is half - way down, some - times ___ when the night ___

___ is dy - ing, I take me out ___ and I wan - der 'round. _____

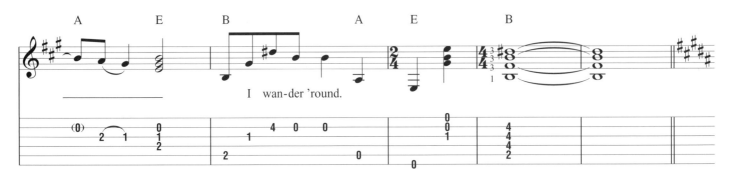

I wan-der 'round.

Outro

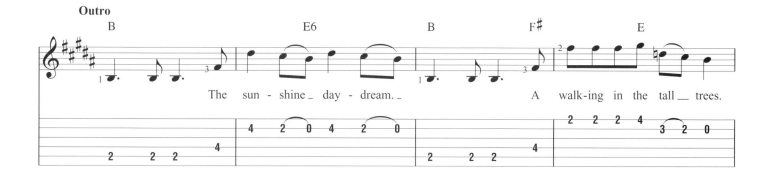

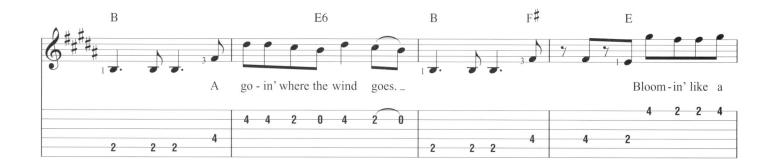

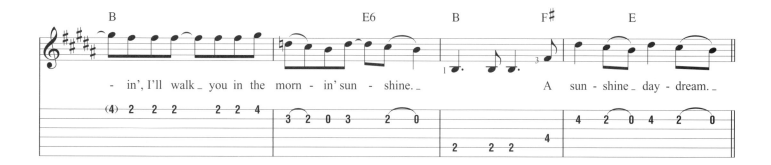

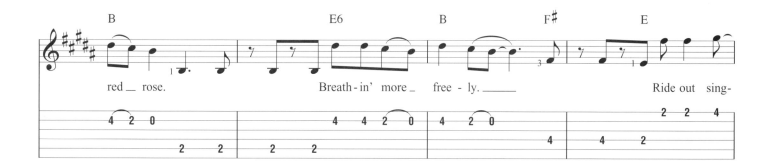

Repeat and fade

Touch of Grey

Words and Music by Jerry Garcia and Robert Hunter

*Tune down 1/2 step:
(low to high) Eb-Ab-Db-Gb-Bb-Eb

Strum Pattern: 3
Pick Pattern: 3

Intro
Fast

*Optional: to match recording, tune down 1/2 step.

1., 2.   3.   % Verse

1. It must be get - ting ear - ly,
2. I see you've got __ your list out.
3. *Guitar Solo*
4., 5. *See additional lyrics*

clocks are run - ning late.   Paint by num - ber morn - ing sky, __
Say your peace __ and get out.   Yes, I get the gist __ of it, __ but

looks so pho - ney.   Dawn is break - ing ev - 'ry - where.
it's al - right. __   Sor - ry that __ you feel that way.

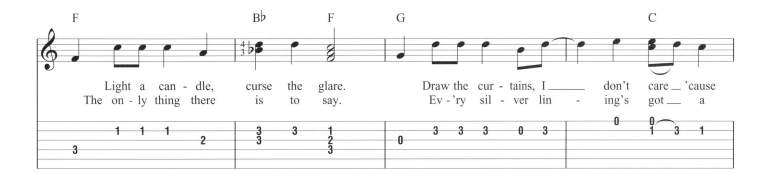

Light a can - dle,   curse the glare.   Draw the cur - tains, I _____ don't care _ 'cause
The on - ly thing there   is to say.   Ev - 'ry sil - ver lin - ing's got _ a

Chorus

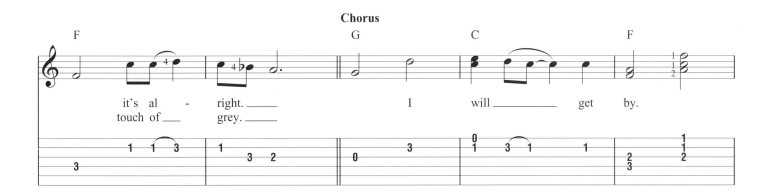

it's al - right. _____   I will _____ get by.
touch of _ grey. _____

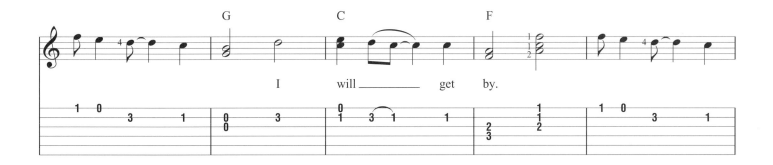

I will _____ get by.

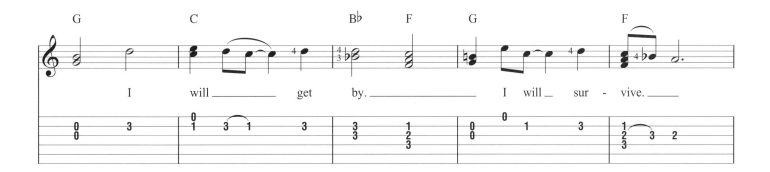

I will _____ get by. _____ I will _ sur - vive. _____

5th time, To Coda 2   **1.**   **2.**

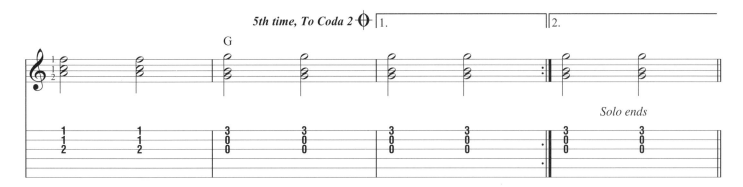

Solo ends

Bridge

It's a les - son _____ that you need. _____ The
It's a les - son _____ to me. _____ The

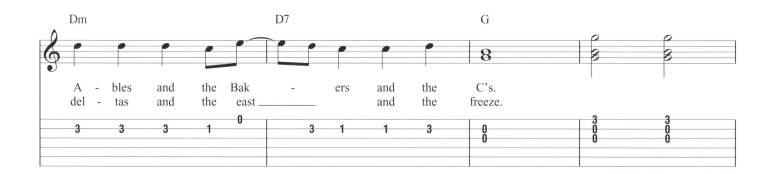

A - bles and the Bak - ers and the C's.
del - tas and the east _____ and the freeze.

The A B C's _____ we all _____ must face _____
The A B C's _____ we all _____ think of _____

To Coda 1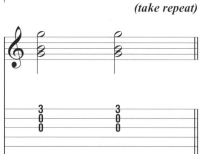

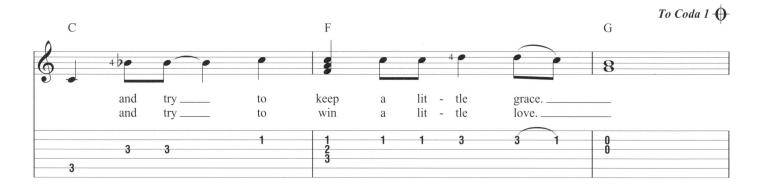

and try _____ to keep a lit - tle grace. _____
and try _____ to win a lit - tle love. _____

D.S. al Coda 1
(take 2nd ending)

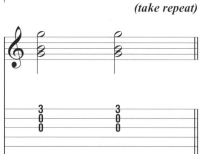 **Coda 1**

D.S. al Coda 2
(take repeat)

 **Coda 2**

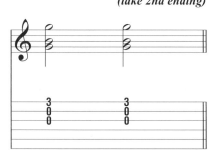

Outro-Chorus

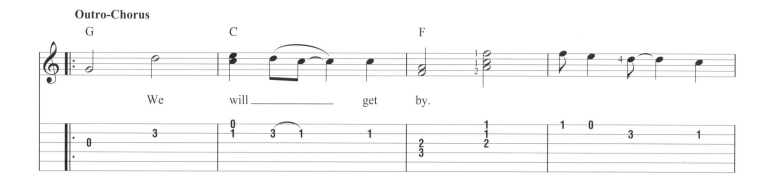

We will _____ get by.

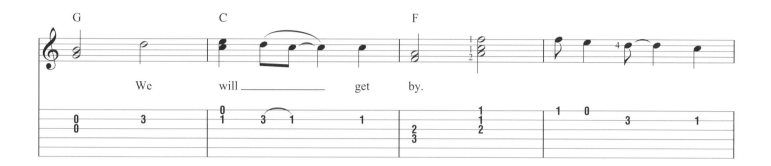

We will _____ get by.

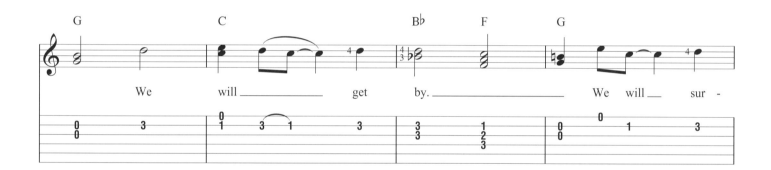

We will _____ get by. _____ We will _ sur -

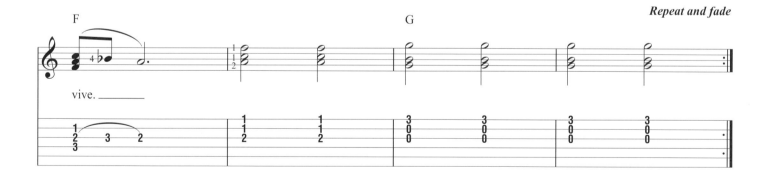

Repeat and fade

vive. _____

Additional Lyrics

3. I know the rent is in arrears,
   The dog has not been fed in years.
   It's even worse than it appears,
   But it's alright.
   Cows giving kerosene,
   Kid can't read at seventeen.
   The words he knows are all obscene,
   But it's alright.

4. The shoe is on the hand, it fits.
   There's really nothing much to it.
   Whistle through your teeth and spit 'cause
   It's alright.
   Oh, well, a touch of grey,
   Kinda suits you anyway.
   That was all I had to say,
   And it's alright.

Casey Jones

Words by Robert Hunter
Music by Jerry Garcia

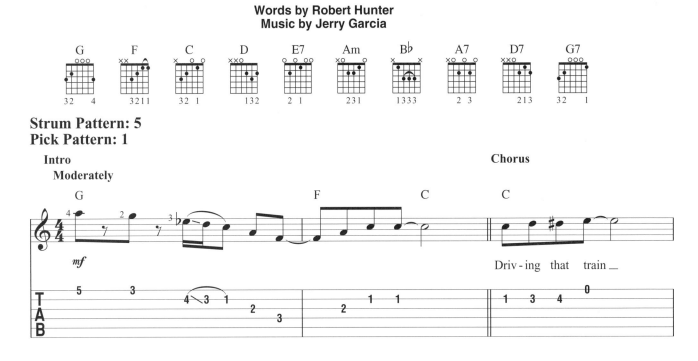

Strum Pattern: 5
Pick Pattern: 1

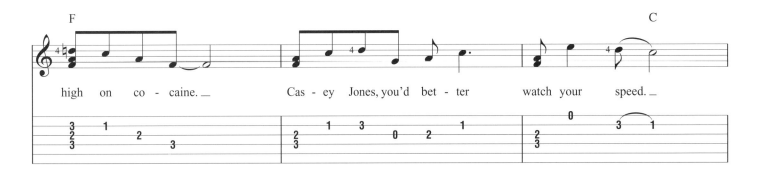

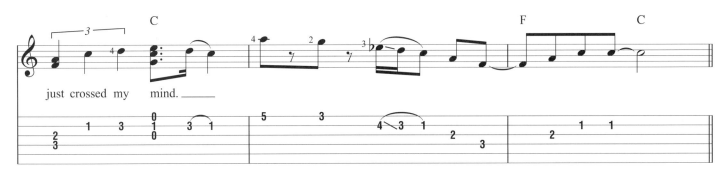

Verse

1. This old en - gine makes it on time, __ leaves Cen - tral Sta - tion 'bout a
2., 4. *See additional lyrics*
3. *Instrumental*

quar - ter to nine. __ Hits Riv - er Junc - tion at sev - en - teen to. __ At a

𝄋 **Chorus**

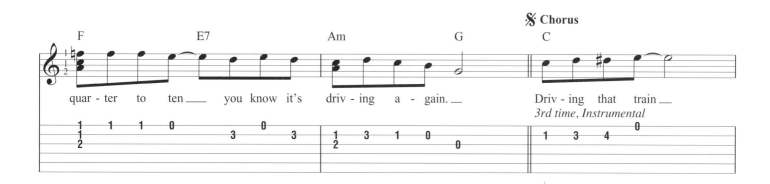

quar - ter to ten __ you know it's driv - ing a - gain. __ Driv - ing that train __
3rd time, Instrumental

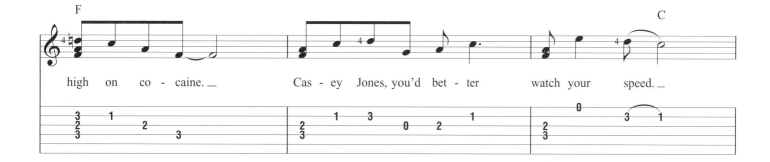

high on co - caine. __ Cas - ey Jones, you'd bet - ter watch your speed. __

5th time, To Coda ⊕

Trou - ble a - head, __ trou - ble be - hind. __ And you know that no - tion

Additional Lyrics

2. Trouble ahead, the lady in red.
   Take my advice, you'd be better off dead.
   Switchman's sleeping, train hundred and two
   Is on the wrong track and headed for you.

4. Trouble with you is the trouble with me.
   Got two good eyes but we still don't see.
   Come 'round the bend, you know it's the end.
   The fireman screams and the engine just gleams.

Friend of the Devil

Words and Music by Jerry Garcia and Robert Hunter

Strum Pattern: 3
Pick Pattern: 3

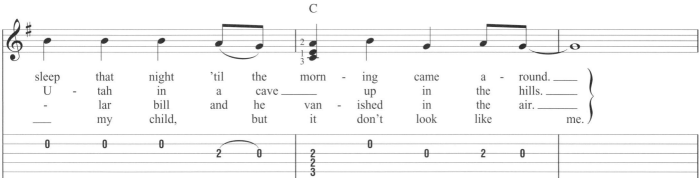

Set out run-ning but I take my time, a friend of the dev-il is a

friend of mine. (If) I get home ___ be - fore ___ day - light,

6th time, To Coda

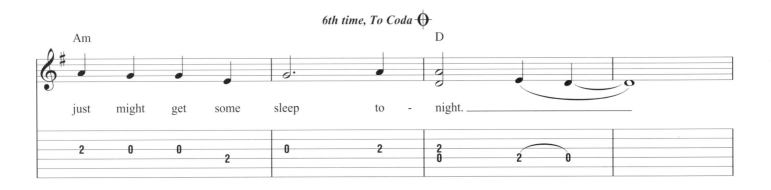

just might get some sleep to - night. _____

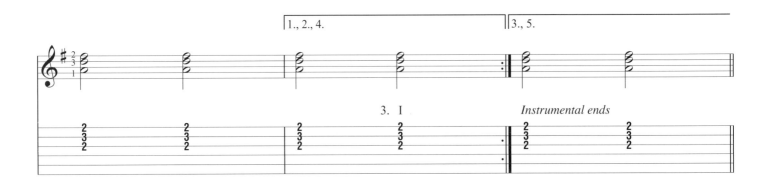

1., 2., 4.   3., 5.

3. I   Instrumental ends

Bridge

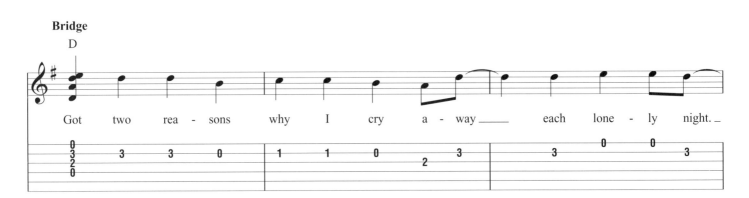

Got two rea - sons why I cry a - way ___ each lone - ly night. _

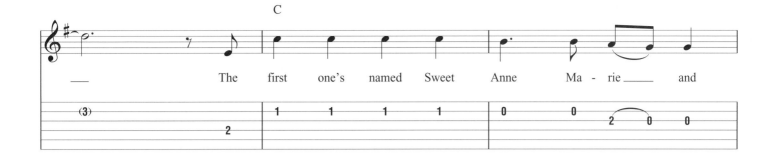

The first one's named Sweet Anne Ma - rie ____ and

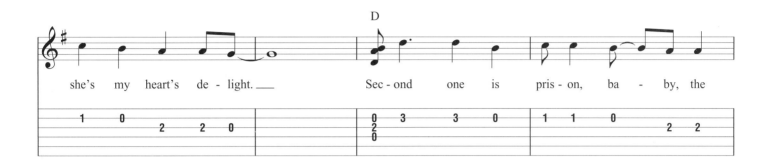

she's my heart's de - light. ____ Sec - ond one is pris - on, ba - by, the

sher - iff's on ____ my trail. And if he catch - es

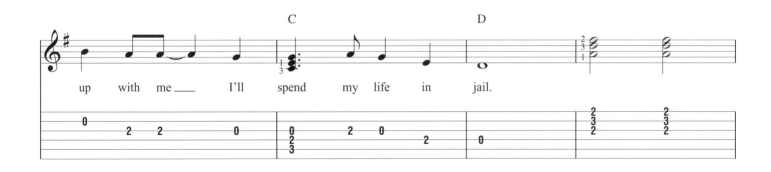

up with me ____ I'll spend my life in jail.

1st time, D.S.
2nd time, D.S. al Coda

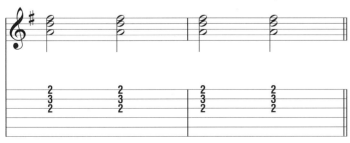

Coda

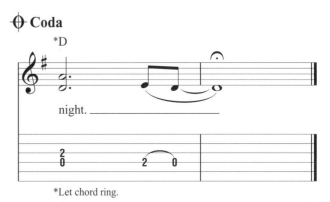

night. ____

*Let chord ring.

Uncle John's Band

Words and Music by Jerry Garcia and Robert Hunter

*Strum Pattern: 3
*Pick Pattern: 3

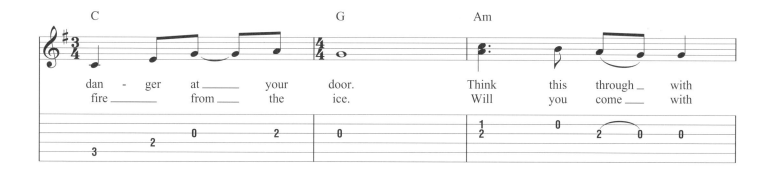

C   G   Am

dan - ger   at _____   your   door.   Think   this   through _ with
fire _____   from _____   the   ice.   Will   you   come _ with

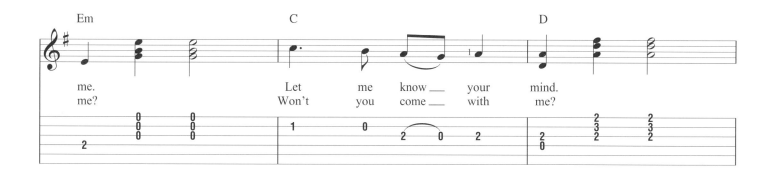

Em   C   D

me.   Let   me   know ___   your   mind.
me?   Won't   you   come ___   with   me?

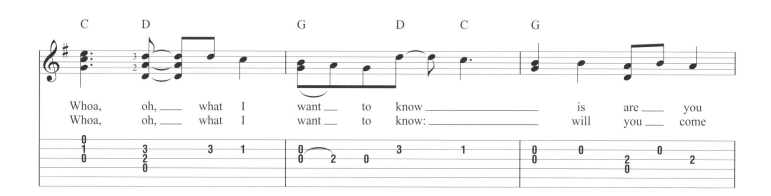

C   D   G   D   C   G

Whoa,   oh, __   what   I   want _   to   know   is   are _   you
Whoa,   oh, __   what   I   want __   to   know: __   will   you _   come

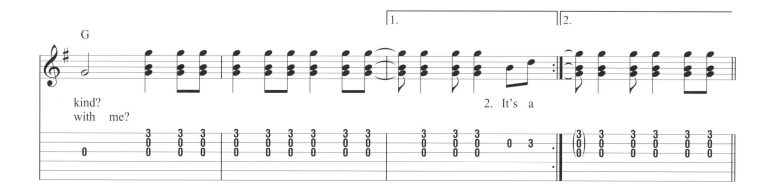

1.   2.

G

kind?
with me?   2. It's a

𝄋 𝄋 **Chorus**

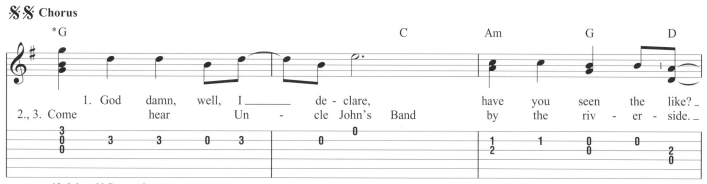

*G   C   Am   G   D

               1. God   damn,   well,   I _____   de - clare,   have   you   seen   the   like? _
2., 3. Come   hear   Un - cle John's Band   by   the   riv - er - side. _

*3rd time, N.C., next 8 meas.

2nd time, To Coda 1 ⊕

3rd time, To Coda 2 ⊕

D.S. al Coda 1
(take repeat)

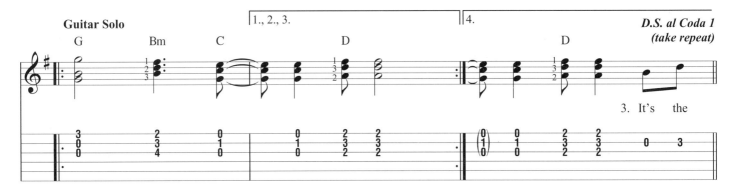

Coda 1

Interlude

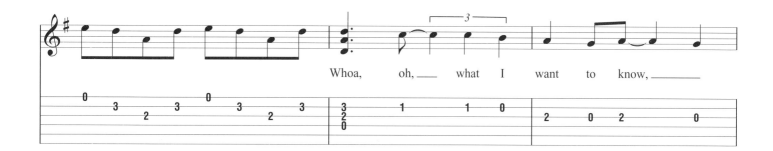

Whoa, oh,___ what I want to know,___

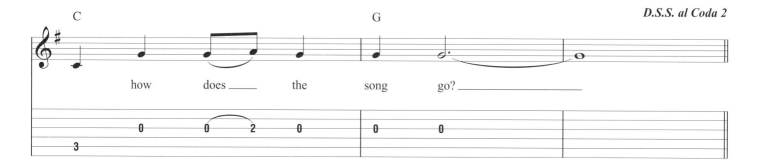

D.S.S. al Coda 2

how does ___ the song go? ___

Coda 2

Outro

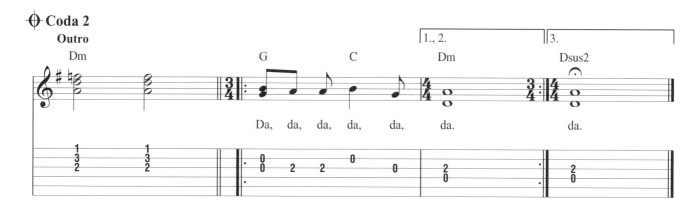

Da, da, da, da, da, da.   da.

Additional Lyrics

3. It's the same story the crow told me,
   It's the only one he knows.
   Like the morning sun, you come,
   And like the wind, you go.
   Ain't no time to hate,
   Barely time to wait.
   Whoa, oh, what I want to know:
   Where does the time go?

4. I live in a silver mine
   And I call it Beggar's Tomb.
   I got me a violin
   And I beg you call the tune.
   Anybody's choice,
   I can hear your voice.
   Whoa, oh, what I want to know:
   How does the song go?

Franklin's Tower

Words and Music by Jerry Garcia, Robert Hunter and Bill Kreutzmann

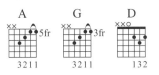

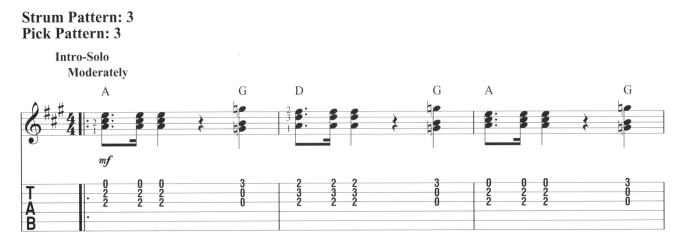

Strum Pattern: 3
Pick Pattern: 3

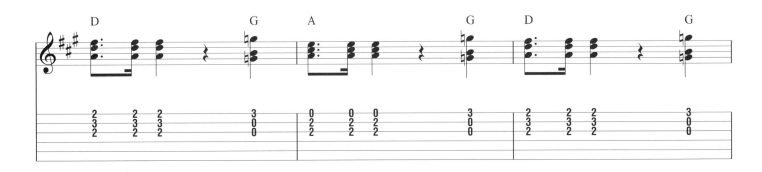

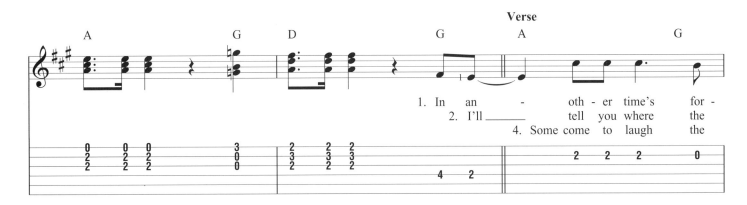

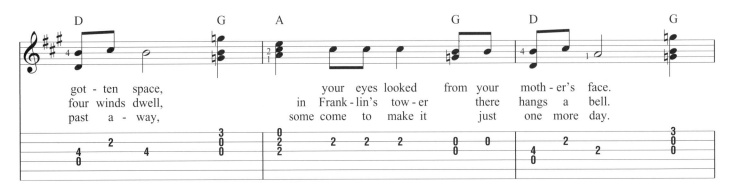

Wild-flow-er seed on the sand and stone, may the four winds blow_ you
It can ring, turn night to day, it can ring like fi-re when_ you
Which-ev-er way your pleas-ure tends, if you plant ice, you gon-na

Chorus

safe-ly home. Roll a-way the dew. _____
lose your way.
har-vest wind.

Roll a-way the dew. _____ Roll a-way the

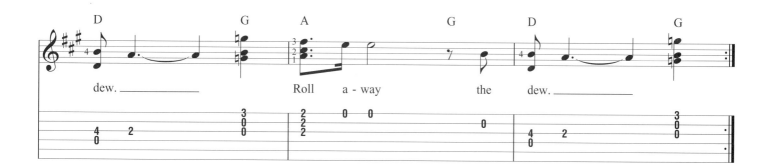

dew. _____ Roll a-way the dew. _____

Verse

3. God save the child who rings that bell, it may have one good ring, ba-by,
5. In Frank-lin's tow-er the four winds sleep, like four lean hounds the

29

you can't tell.
light-house keep.
One watch by night,
Wild-flow - er seed on the
one watch by day.
sand and wind,

To Coda ⊕

D.C. al Coda
(no repeat)

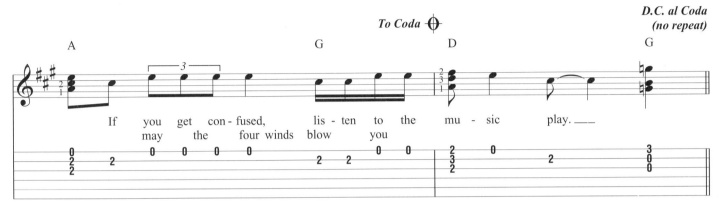

If you get con - fused, lis - ten to the mu - sic play. ___
may the four winds blow you

⊕ **Coda**

Outro-Chorus

home a - gain.
Roll a - way
the dew. ___

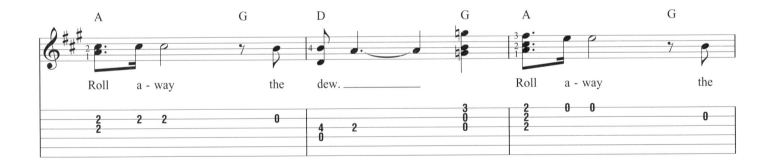

Roll a - way
the dew. ___
Roll a - way
the

Repeat and fade

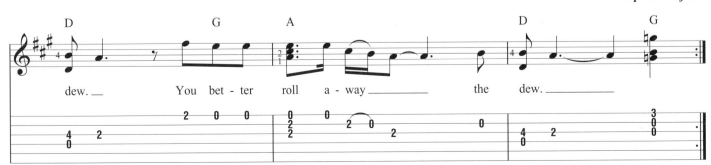

dew. __
You bet - ter roll a - way ___
the dew. ___

Estimated Prophet

Words and Music by Bob Weir and John Barlow

My time com-in', voic-es say - in', __ they tell me where to go.
Still, I know I lead the way, _____ they tell me where I go.
My time com-in' an - y day, _____ don't wor-ry a - bout __ me, no.
Don't

Pre-Chorus

3rd time, To Coda

wor-ry a - bout __ me, oh, nah, nah, __ don't wor-ry a - bout __ me, no.
And I'm

in no hur - ry, hah, nah, nah, nah, I know where to go.
Cal - i -

Chorus

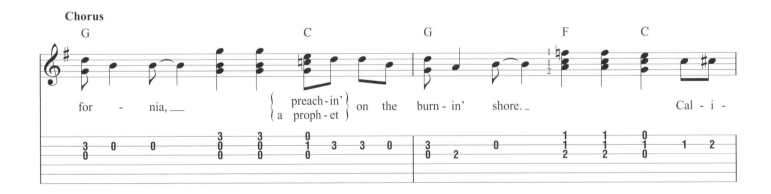

for - nia, __ preach-in' / a proph-et } on the burn - in' shore. __
Cal - i -

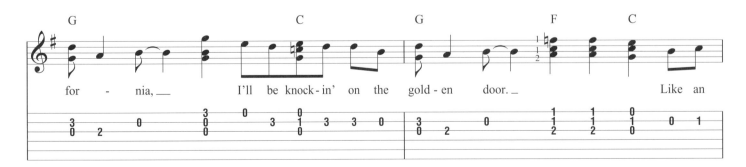

for - nia, __ I'll be knock-in' on the gold - en door. __
Like an

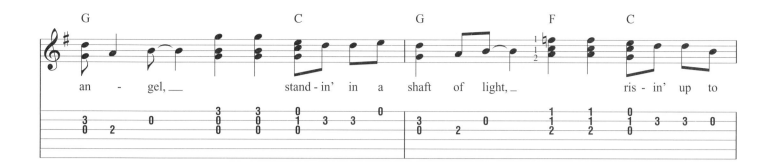

an - gel, ___ stand - in' in a shaft of light, ___ ris - in' up to

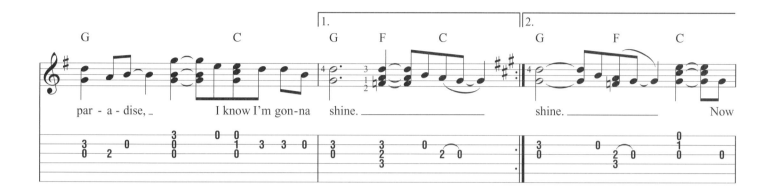

par - a - dise, ___ I know I'm gon-na shine. ___ shine. ___ Now

you've all been a - sleep, ___ you would not be - lieve me. ___ (Oo.) ___ And them

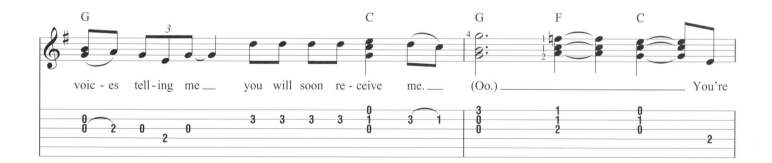

voic - es tell-ing me ___ you will soon re - ceive me. ___ (Oo.) ___ You're

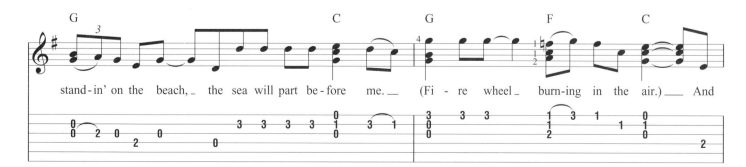

stand - in' on the beach, ___ the sea will part be - fore me. ___ (Fi - re wheel ___ burn-ing in the air.) ___ And

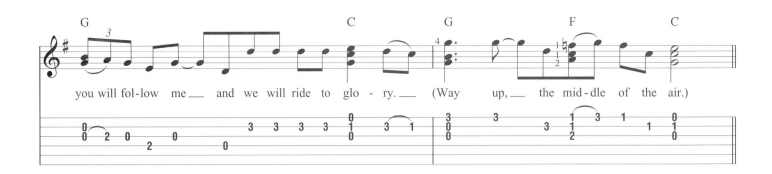

you will fol-low me ___ and we will ride to glo - ry. ___ (Way up, ___ the mid - dle of the air.)

Bridge

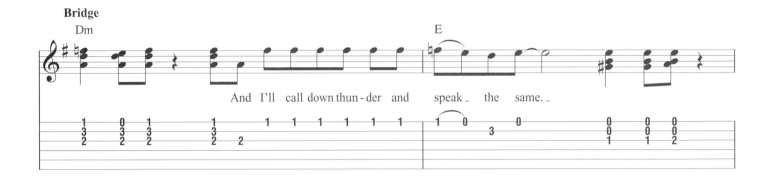

And I'll call down thun - der and speak ___ the same. ___

And my work fills the sky ___ with flame. ___

And might and glo - ry gon-na be my name. _____

And men gon-na light my way. _____

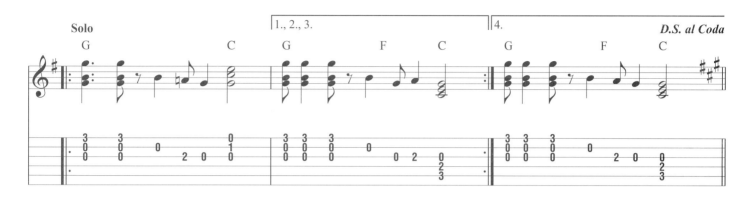

Eyes of the World

Words and Music by Jerry Garcia and Robert Hunter

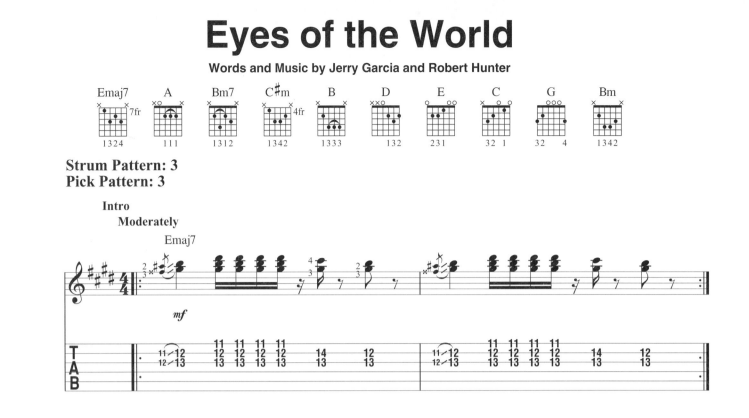

Strum Pattern: 3
Pick Pattern: 3

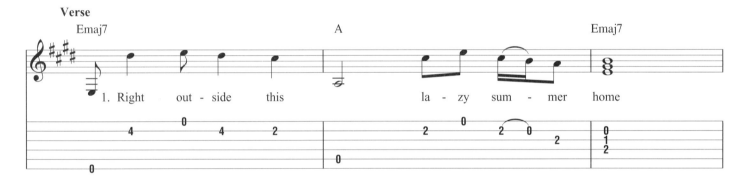

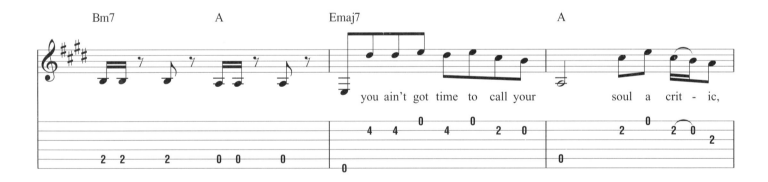

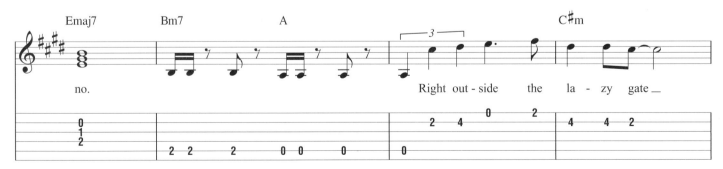

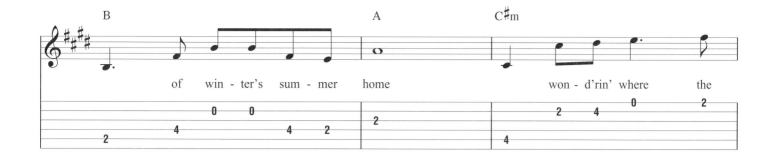

of win-ter's sum-mer home　　　won-d'rin' where the

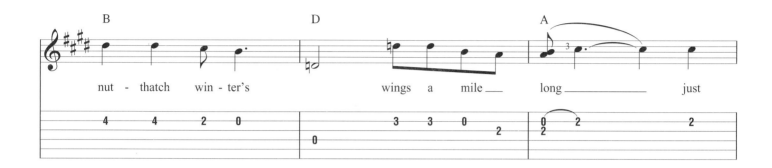

nut-thatch win-ter's　　wings a mile　long　just

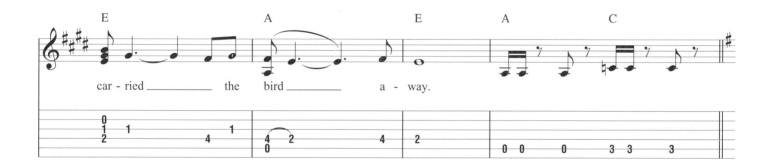

car-ried　the bird　a-way.

𝄋 Chorus

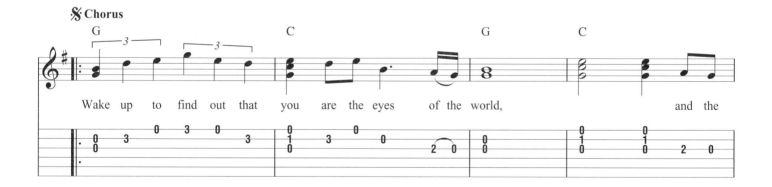

Wake up to find out that you are the eyes of the world,　　and the

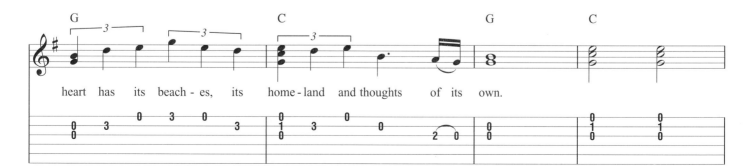

heart has its beach-es,　its home-land and thoughts of its own.

Wake now, dis-cov-er that you are the song that the morn-in' brings. _ The

3rd time, To Coda ⊕

heart has its sea-sons, its eve-nin's and songs of its own.

Guitar Solo

*2nd time, substitute A.

**2nd time, substitute A.

Verse

comes a re-deem-er and he slow-ly too fades a-way,
3. Some-times we live no par-tic-u-lar way but our own,

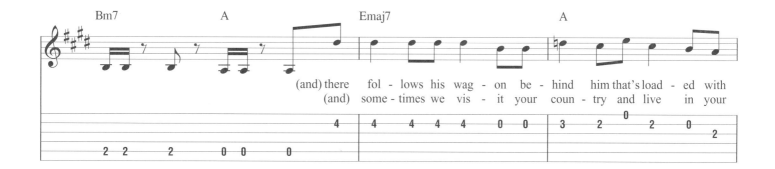

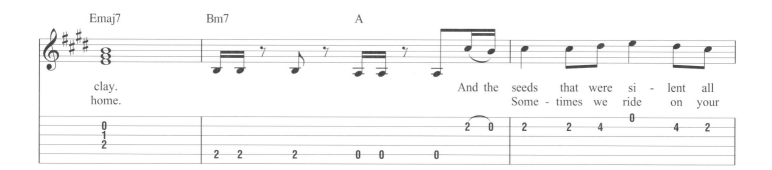

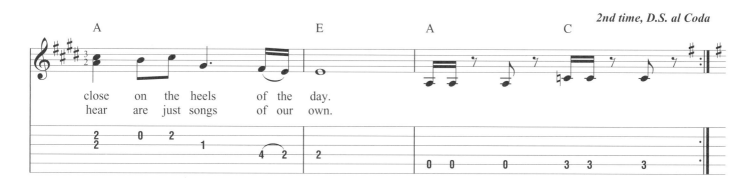

⊕ Coda

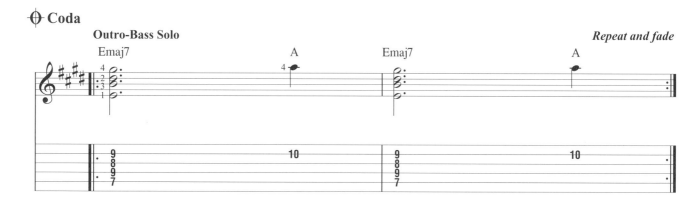

Box of Rain

Words and Music by Robert Hunter and Phil Lesh

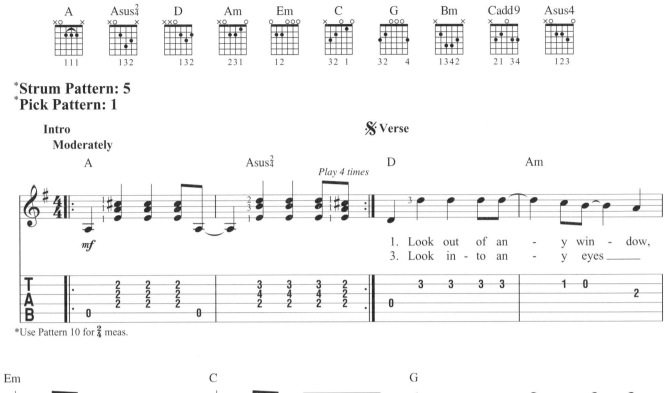

*Strum Pattern: 5
*Pick Pattern: 1

*Use Pattern 10 for 2/4 meas.

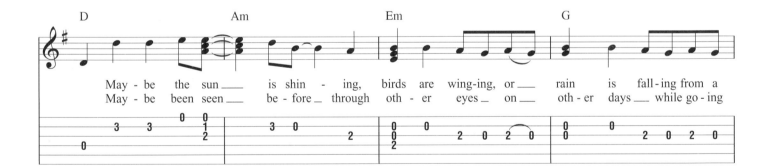

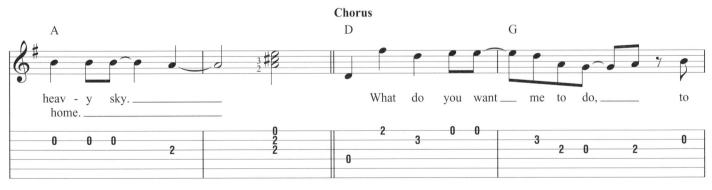

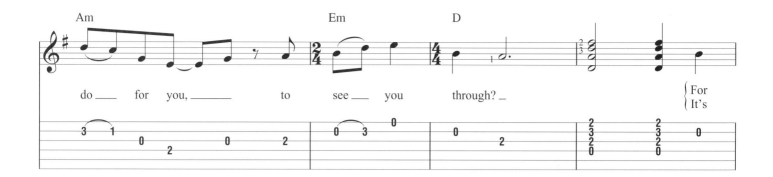

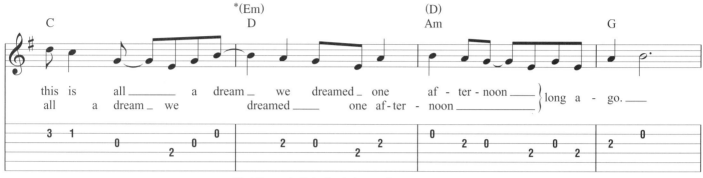

*2nd time, substitute chords in parentheses.

Verse

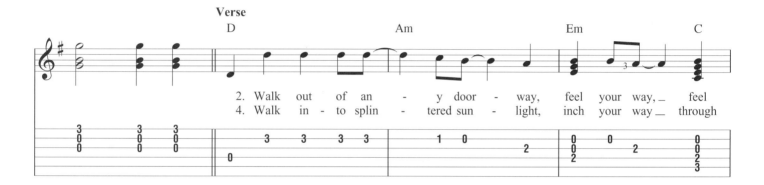

Chorus

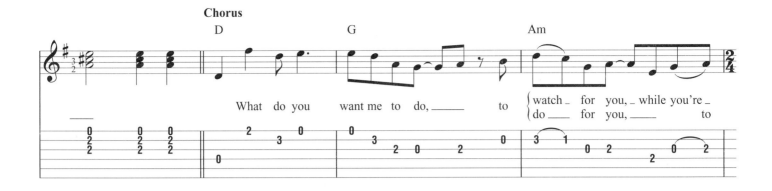

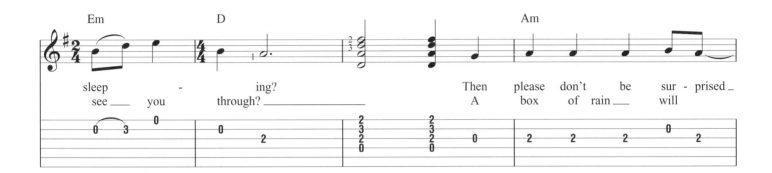

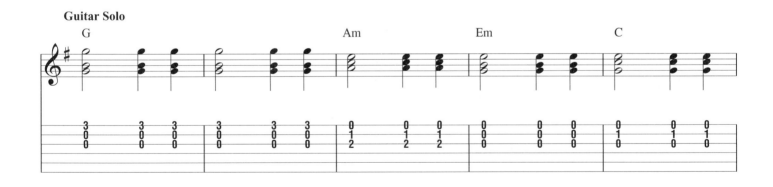

Guitar Solo

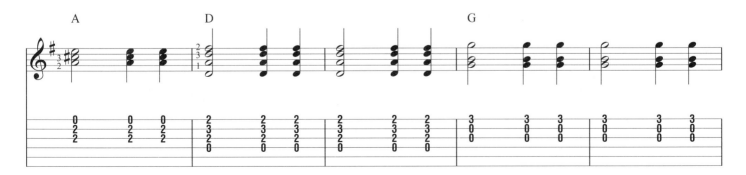

42

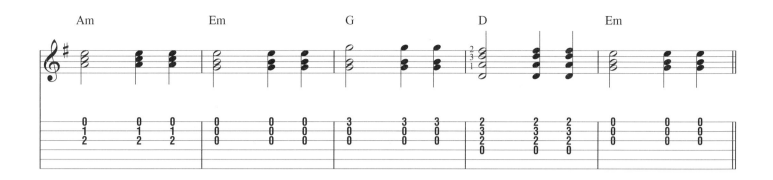

2nd time, D.S. al Coda

⊕ Coda

Bridge

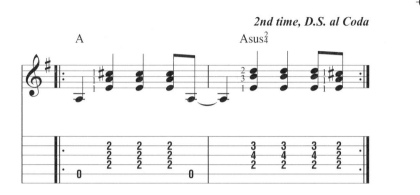

Just a box of rain, _____

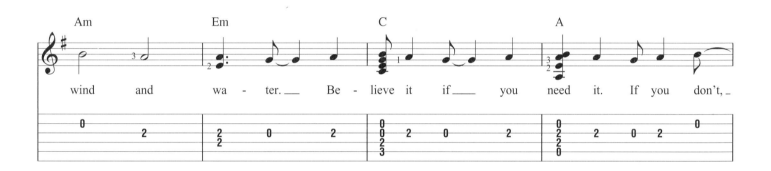

wind and wa - ter. ___ Be - lieve it if ___ you need it. If you don't, ___

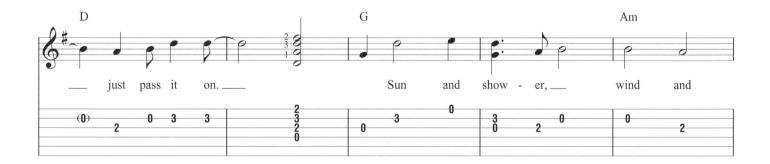

___ just pass it on. ___ Sun and show - er, ___ wind and

rain. ___ In and out ___ the win - dow like a moth ___ be - fore a

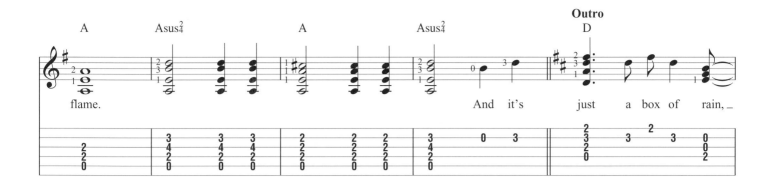

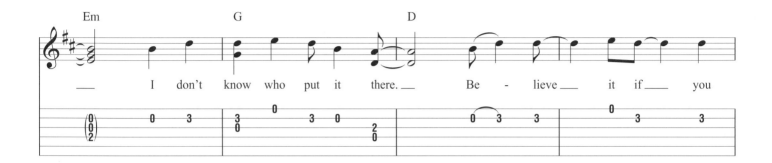

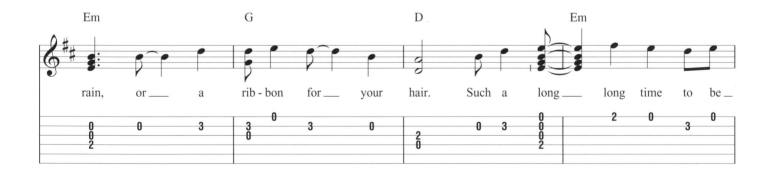

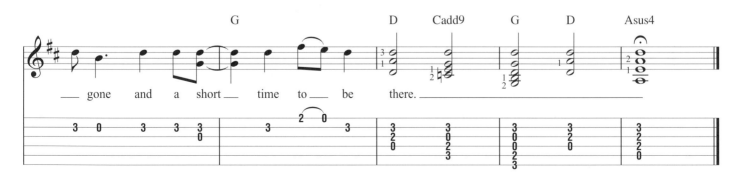

The Golden Road

Words and Music by Jerry Garcia, Bill Kreutzmann, Phil Lesh, Ron McKernan and Bob Weir

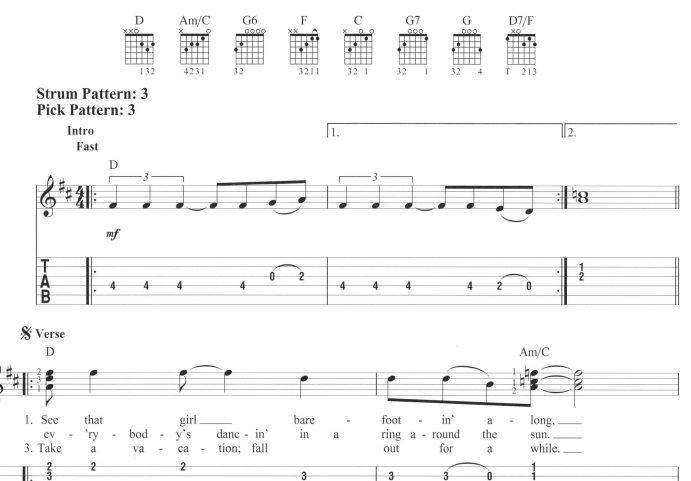

Strum Pattern: 3
Pick Pattern: 3

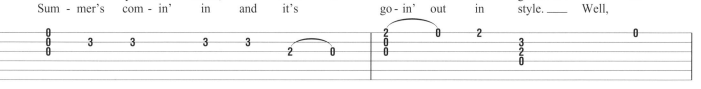

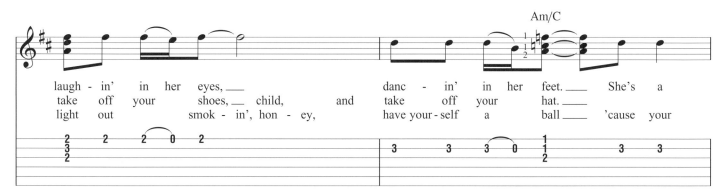

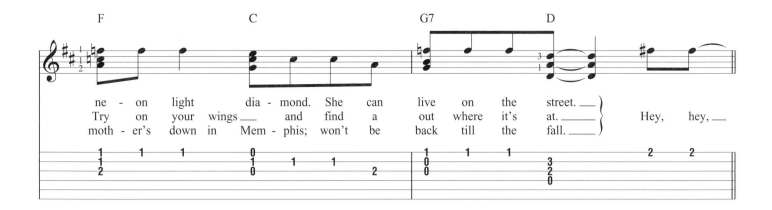

ne - on light dia - mond. She can live on the street. ⌉
Try on your wings ___ and find a out where it's at. ___ ⎬ Hey, hey, ___
moth - er's down in Mem - phis; won't be back till the fall. ___ ⌋

Chorus

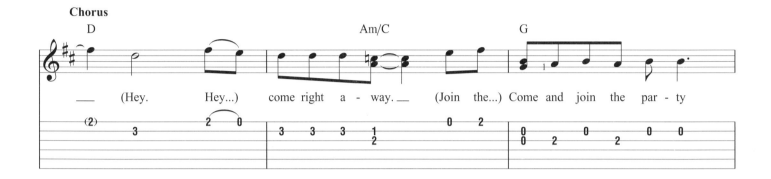

___ (Hey. Hey...) come right a - way. ___ (Join the...) Come and join the par - ty

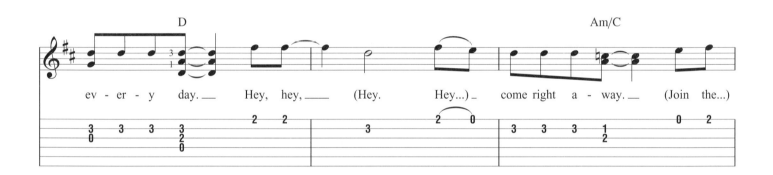

ev - er - y day. ___ Hey, hey, ___ (Hey. Hey...) ___ come right a - way. ___ (Join the...)

3rd time, To Coda ⊕ | 1. | 2.

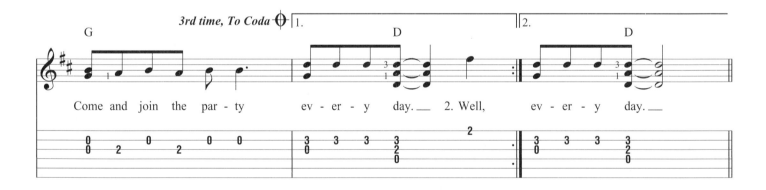

Come and join the par - ty ev - er - y day. ___ 2. Well, ev - er - y day. ___

Guitar Solo   *3rd time, D.S. al Coda*

Play 3 times

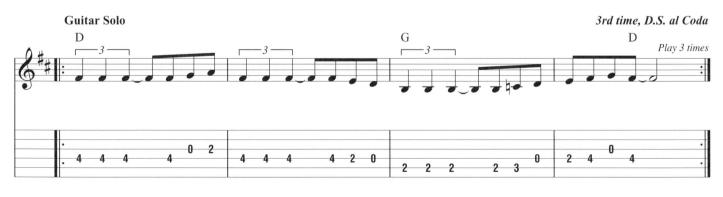

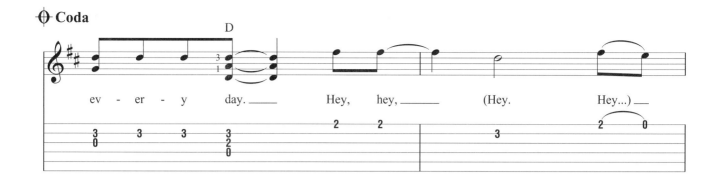

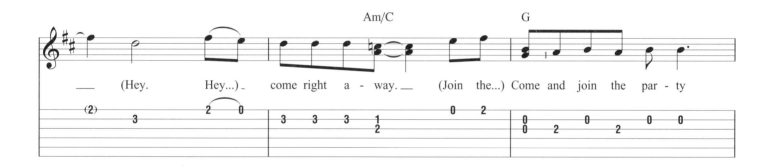

U.S. Blues

Words and Music by Jerry Garcia and Robert Hunter

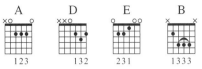

Strum Pattern: 6
Pick Pattern: 6

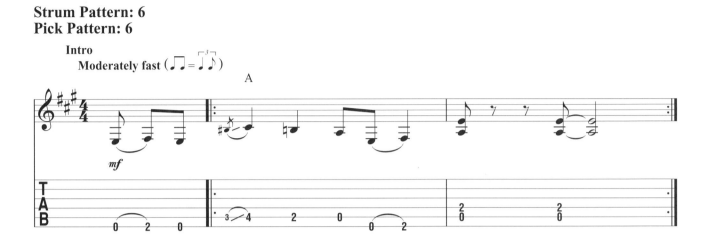

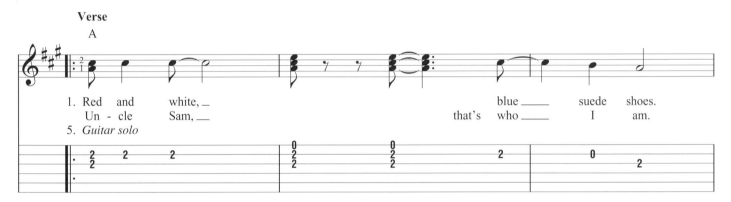

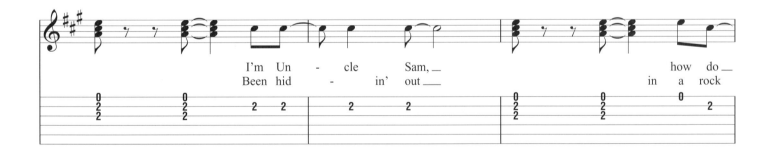

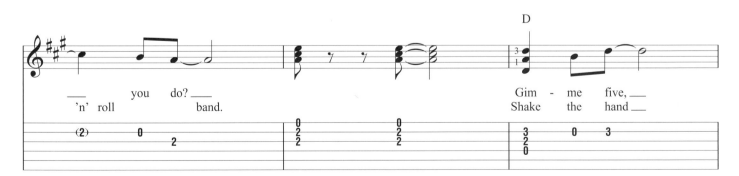

I'm still a - live. ___ Ain't ___
that shook the hand ___ of

___ no luck, I learned to duck. ___
P. T. Bar-num and Char - lie Chan. ___

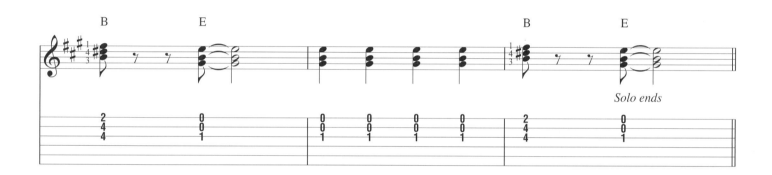

Solo ends

Verse

2. Check my pulse, ___ it _____ don't change. ___
4. Shine your shoes, ___ light the fuse. ___
6. Back to back ___ chick - en shack. ___

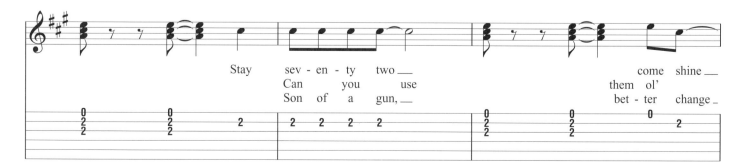

Stay sev - en - ty two ___ come shine ___
Can you use them ol'
Son of a gun, ___ bet - ter change ___

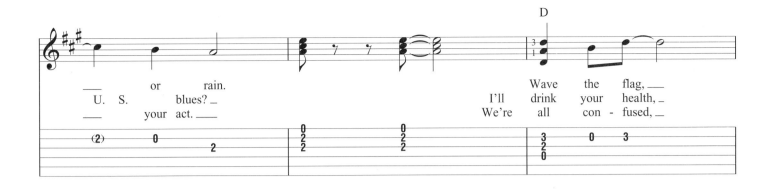

or rain.
U. S.　　　blues?
your act.

Wave　　the　flag,
I'll　drink　your　health,
We're　all　con - fused,

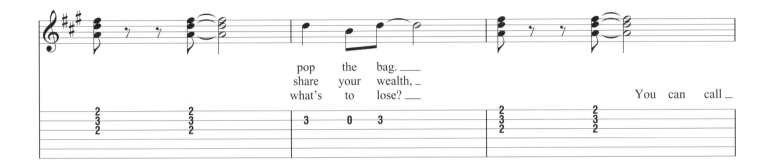

pop　　the　bag.
share　your　wealth,
what's　to　lose?　　　　　　　　　You can call

Rock　the　boat,
run　your　life,
this　song

skin　the　goat.
steal　your　wife.
"The U - nit - ed States Blues."

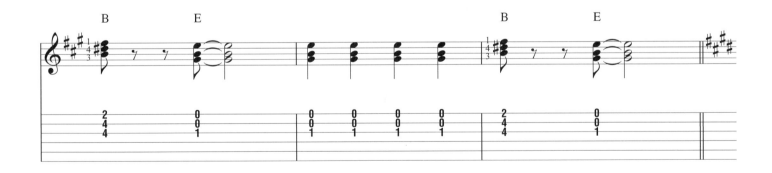

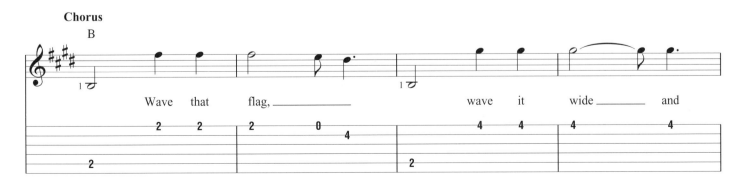

Chorus

Wave　that　flag,　　　　　　　　　wave　it　wide　　　　and

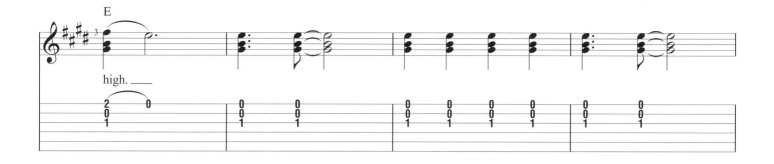

high.

Sum-mer time ___ done ___ come and gone, ___ my, oh,

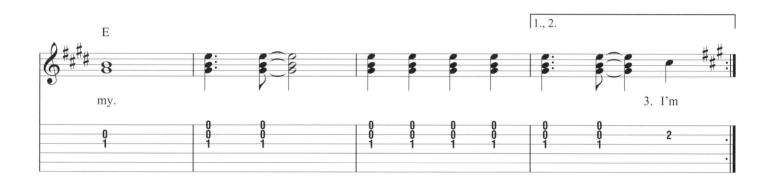

my.

3. I'm

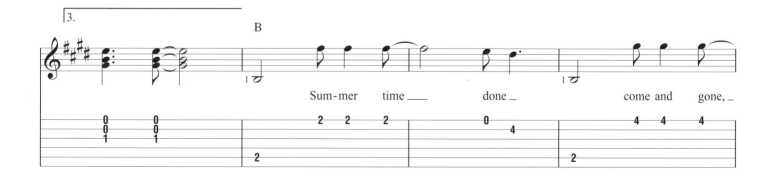

Sum-mer time ___ done ___ come and gone, ___

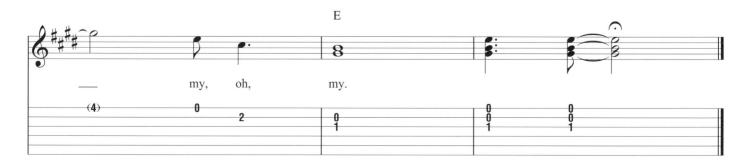

my, oh, my.

One More Saturday Night

Words and Music by Bob Weir

Hey, Sat-ur-day night. ___

Hey, uh, huh, ___

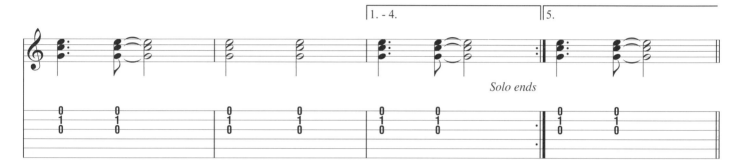

One more Sat-ur-day night. ___

Hey, Sat-ur-day night. ___

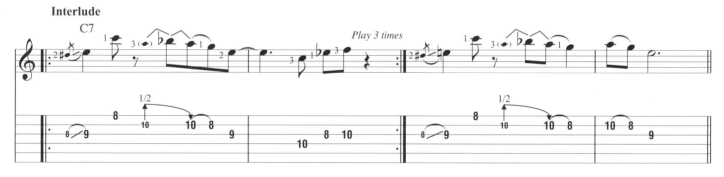

1. - 4.

5.

Solo ends

Interlude

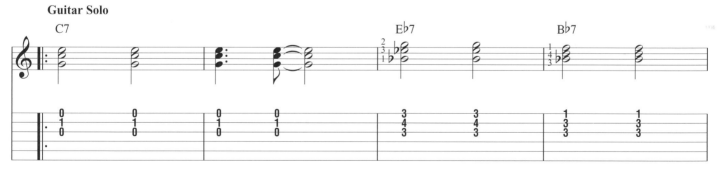

Play 3 times

Guitar Solo

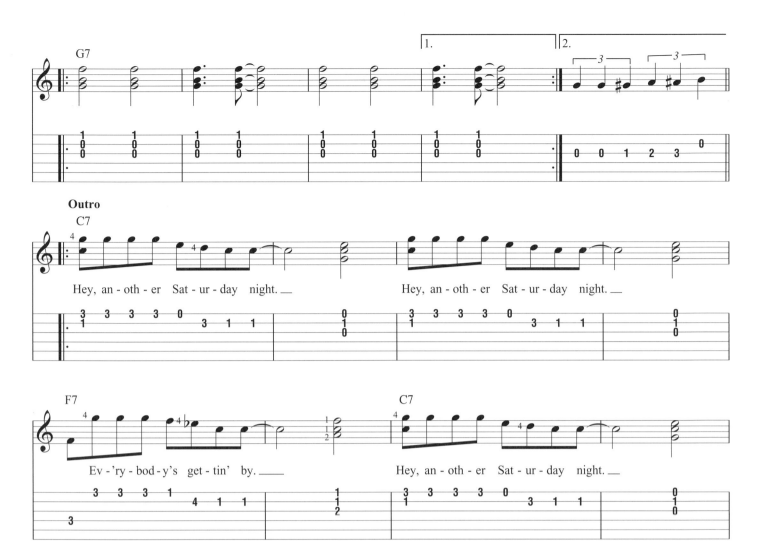

Outro

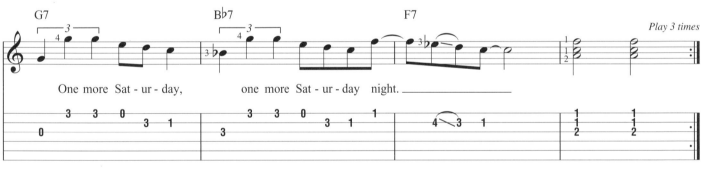

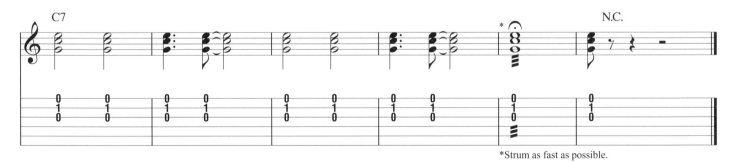

*Strum as fast as possible.

Additional Lyrics

4. Turn on channel six. The president comes on the news.
   Says, "I get no satisfaction. That's why I sing the blues."
   His wife says, "Don't get crazy. Lord, you know just what to do.
   Crank up that old Victrola. Break out your rockin' shoes."

5. Then God way up in heaven, for whatever it was worth,
   Thought He'd have a big ol' party; thought He'd call it planet earth.
   Don't worry about tomorrow. Lord, you'll know it when it comes,
   When the rockin' rollin' music meets the risin', shinin' sun.

Fire on the Mountain

Words and Music by Robert Hunter and Mickey Hart

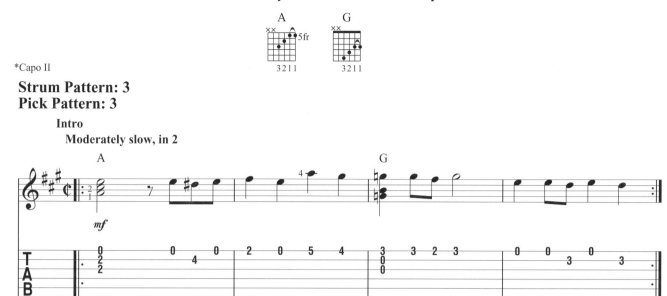

*Capo II

Strum Pattern: 3
Pick Pattern: 3

Intro
Moderately slow, in 2

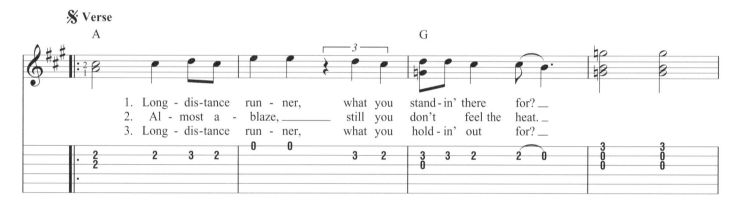

*Optional: To match recording, place capo at 2nd fret.

Verse

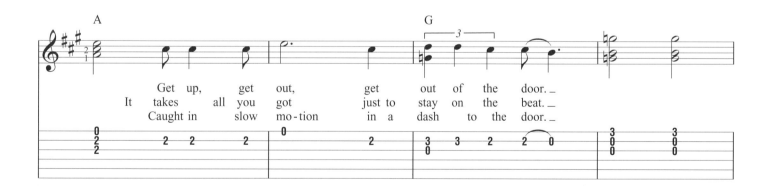

1. Long - dis - tance run - ner, what you stand - in' there for? __
2. Al - most a - blaze, __ still you don't feel the heat. __
3. Long - dis - tance run - ner, what you hold - in' out for? __

Get up, get out, get out of the door. __
It takes all you got just to stay on the beat. __
Caught in slow mo - tion in a dash to the door. __

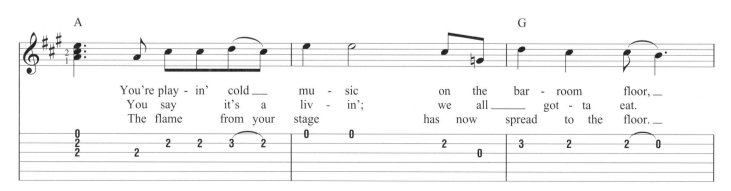

You're play - in' cold __ mu - sic on the bar - room floor, __
You say it's a liv - in'; we all __ got - ta eat. __
The flame from your stage has now spread to the floor. __

drowned in your laugh - ter and
But you're here a - lone; there's no
You gave all you had, why you

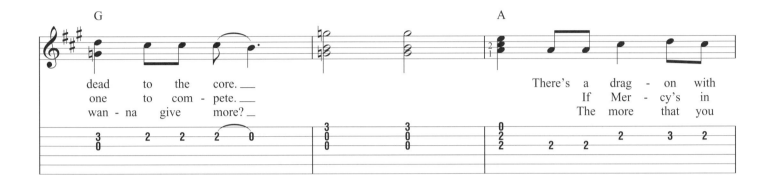

dead to the core.
one to com - pete.
wan - na give more?

There's a drag - on with
If Mer - cy's in
The more that you

match - es that's loose on the town.
busi - ness, I wish it for you.
give the more it will take.

Take a whole pail of
More than just
To the thin line be -

3rd time, To Coda ⊕

wa - ter just to cool him down.
ash - es when your dreams come true.
yond which you real - ly can't fake.

Well,

Chorus

fi - re, fi - re on the moun - tain.

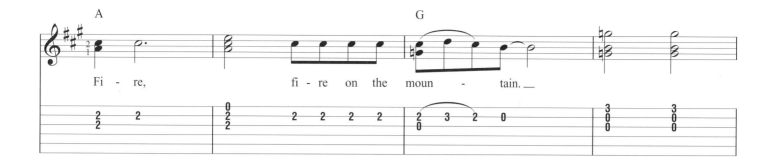

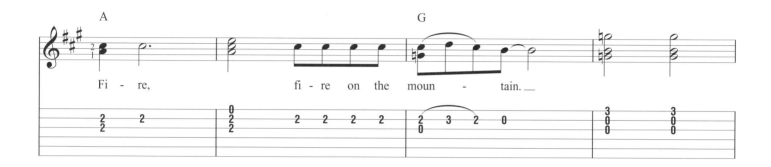

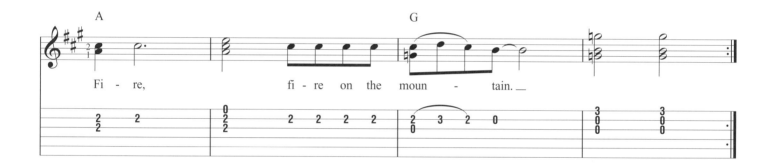

Guitar Solo

1., 2., 3.   4.   *D.S. al Coda*

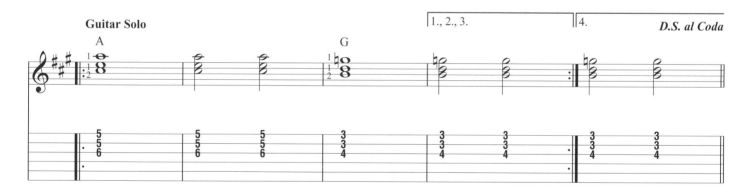

⊕ **Coda**

Outro-Chorus   *Repeat and fade*

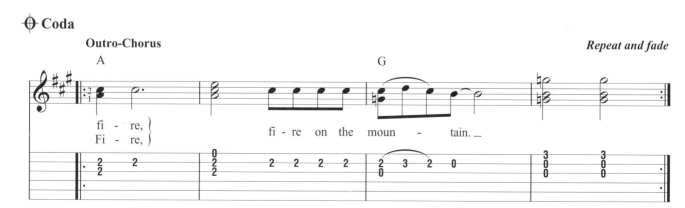

The Music Never Stopped

Words and Music by John Barlow and Bob Weir

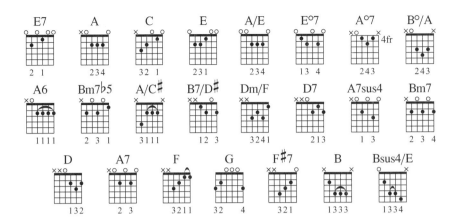

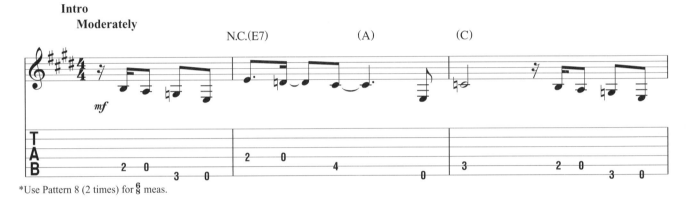

*Strum Pattern: 3
*Pick Pattern: 3

*Use Pattern 8 (2 times) for $\frac{6}{8}$ meas.

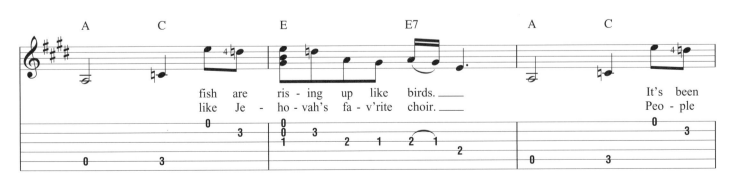

**Use Pattern 10.

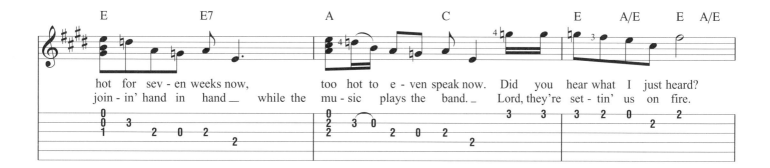

hot for sev - en weeks now, too hot to e - ven speak now. Did you hear what I just heard?
join - in' hand in hand __ while the mu - sic plays the band. __ Lord, they're set - tin' us on fire.

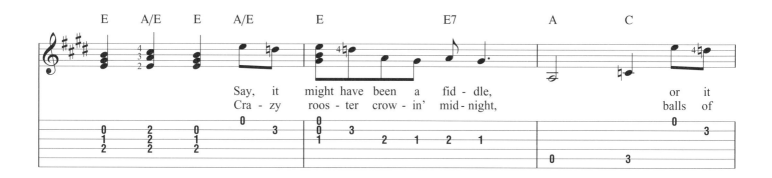

Say, it might have been a fid - dle, or it
Cra - zy roos - ter crow - in' mid - night, balls of

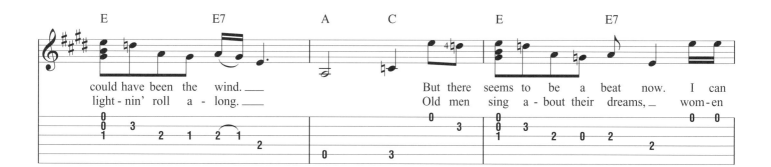

could have been the wind. ___ But there seems to be a beat now. I can
light - nin' roll a - long. ___ Old men sing a - bout their dreams, __ wom - en

feel it in my feet now. Lis - ten, here it comes a - gain.
laugh and chil - dren scream, __ and the band keeps play - in' on.

Bridge

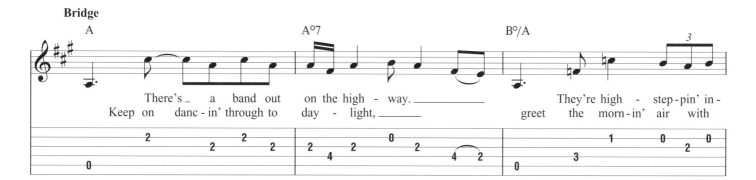

There's __ a band out on the high - way. _____ They're high - step - pin' in -
Keep on danc - in' through to day - light, _____ greet the morn - in' air with

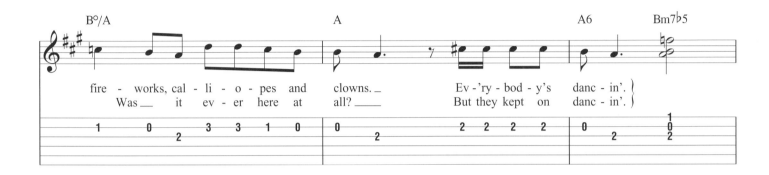

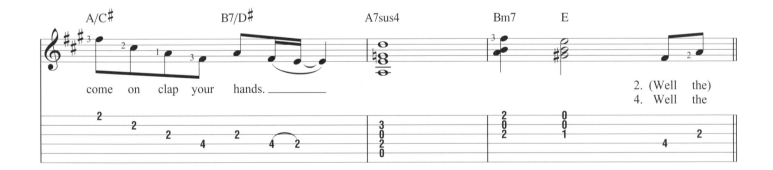

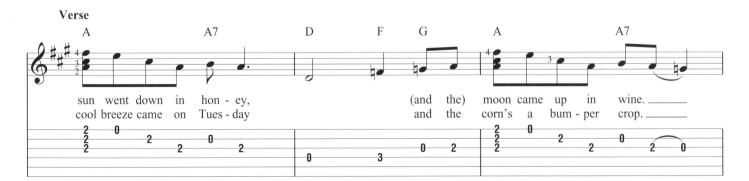

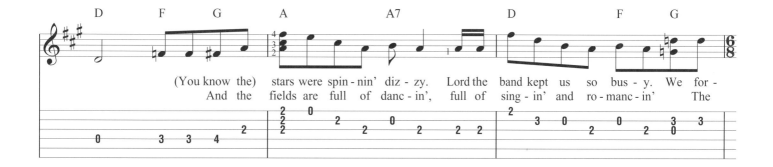

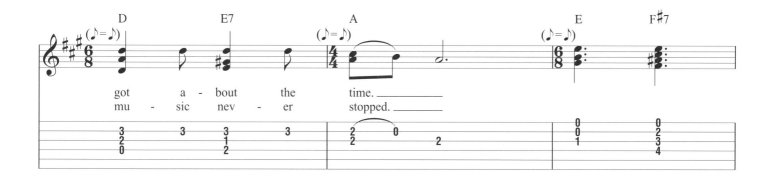

(You know the) stars were spin-nin' diz-zy. Lord the band kept us so bus-y. We for-
And the fields are full of danc-in', full of sing-in' and ro-manc-in' The

got a - bout the time. _____
mu - sic nev - er stopped. _____

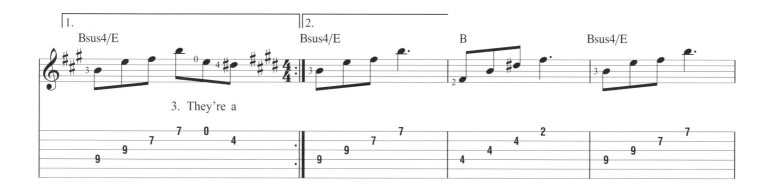

3. They're a

Outro-Solo   *Repeat and fade*

Hell in a Bucket

Words and Music by John Barlow, Brent Mydland and Bob Weir

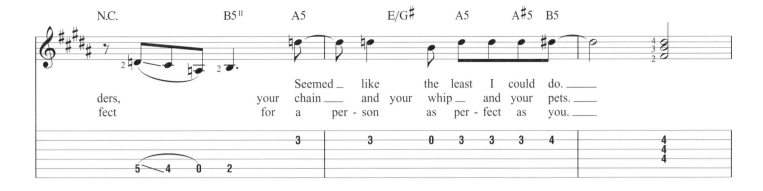

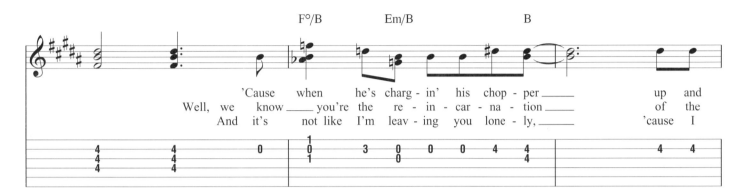

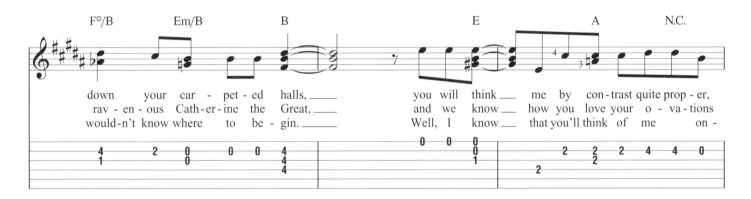

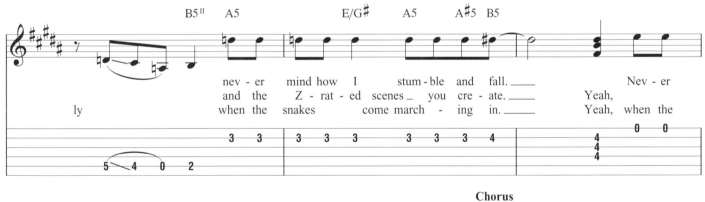

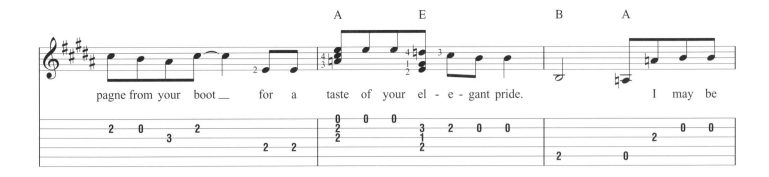

pagne from your boot __ for a taste of your el - e - gant pride.   I may be

3rd time, To Coda 2 ⊕

go - ing to hell in a buck - et, babe, __   but at least I'm en - joy - ing the ride.

At least I'm en - joy - ing the ride.   Yeah, __

To Coda 1 ⊕ **Guitar Solo**

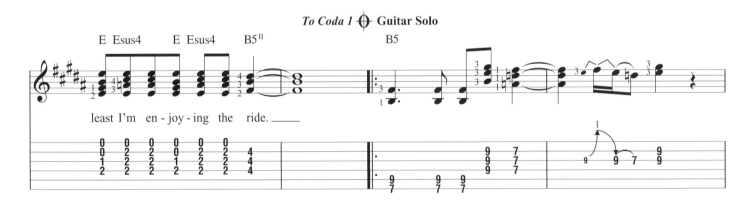

least I'm en - joy - ing the ride. __

1.   2.   *D.S. al Coda 1*

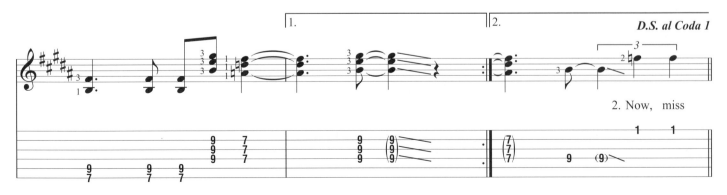

2. Now, miss

Coda 1

Bridge

You an-a-lyze _ me, a, tend to de-spise _ me. You laugh _ when I stum-ble and fall. _

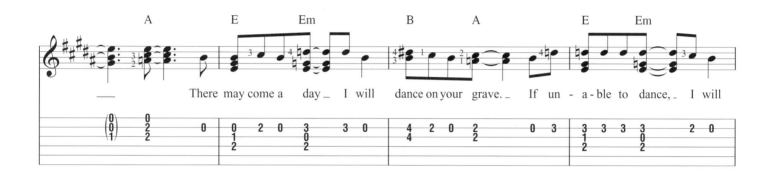

_ There may come a day _ I will dance on your grave. _ If un-a-ble to dance, _ I will

crawl a-cross it. ____ Or un-a-ble to dance, _ I will crawl. Yeah, _ un -

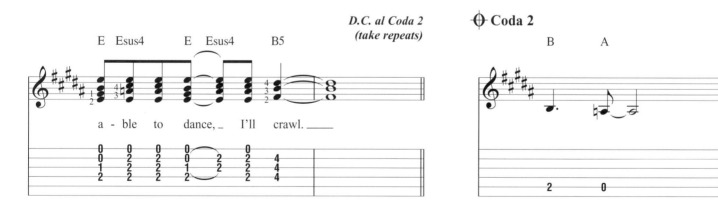

a-ble to dance, _ I'll crawl. ____

D.C. al Coda 2
(take repeats)

Coda 2

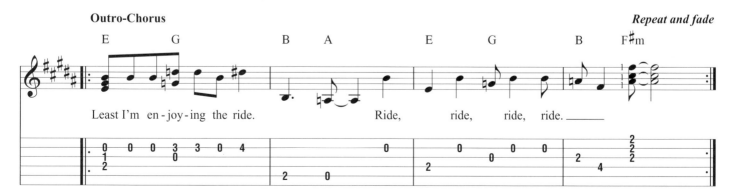

Outro-Chorus

Repeat and fade

Least I'm en-joy-ing the ride. Ride, ride, ride, ride. _____

Ripple

Words and Music by Jerry Garcia and Robert Hunter

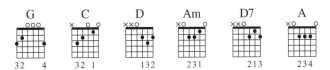

Strum Pattern: 3
Pick Pattern: 3

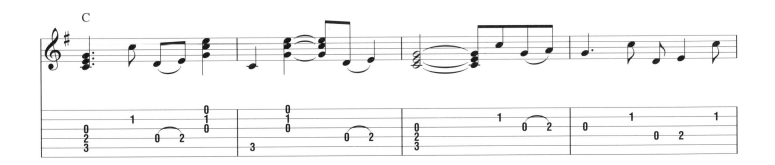

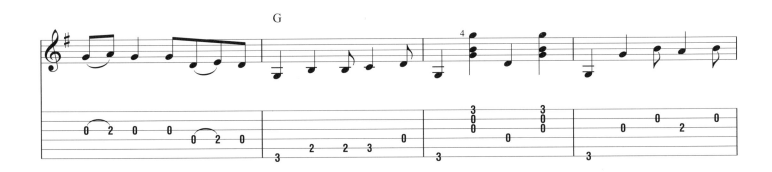

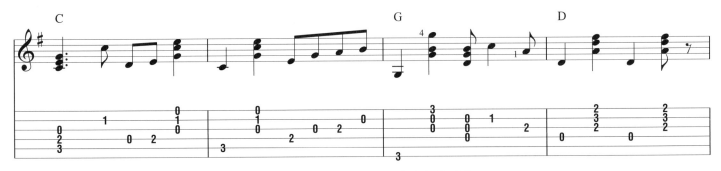

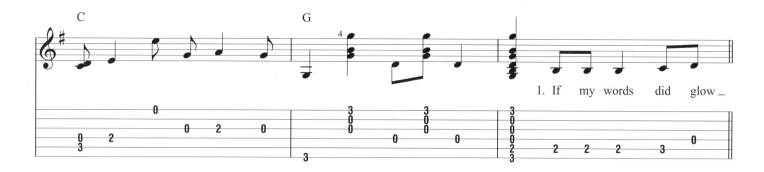

1. If my words did glow __

𝄋 **Verse**

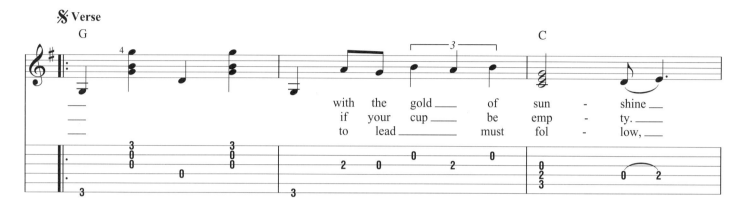

with the gold __ of sun - shine __
if your cup __ be emp - ty. __
to lead __ must fol - low, __

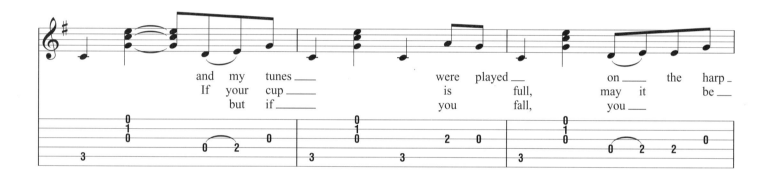

and my tunes __ were played __ on __ the harp __
If your cup __ is full, may it be __
but if __ you fall, you __

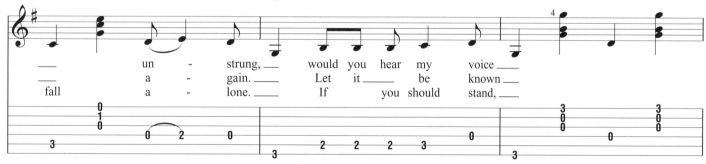

un - strung, __ would you hear my voice __
a - gain. __ Let it __ be known __
fall a - lone. __ If you should stand, __

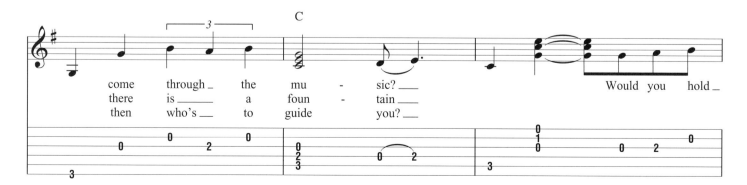

come through the mu - sic? __
there is a foun - tain __
then who's __ to guide you? __

Would you hold __

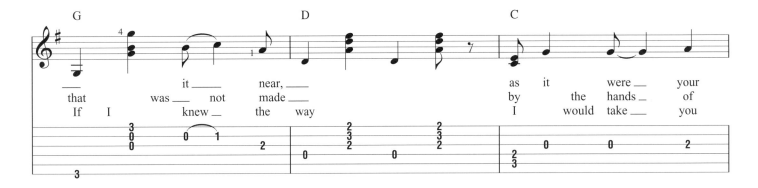

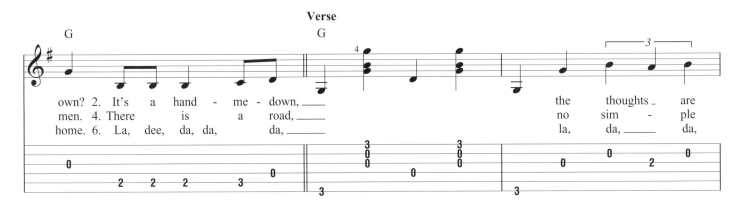

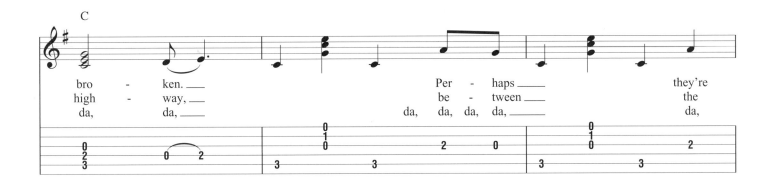

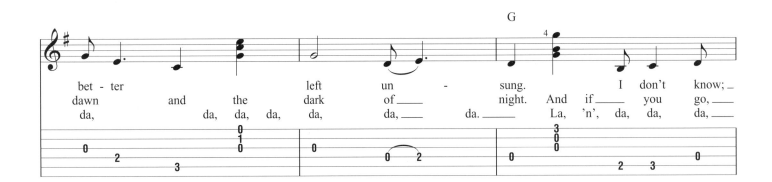

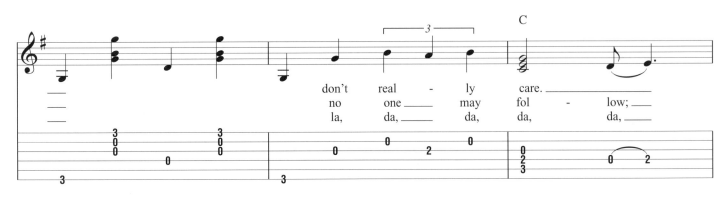

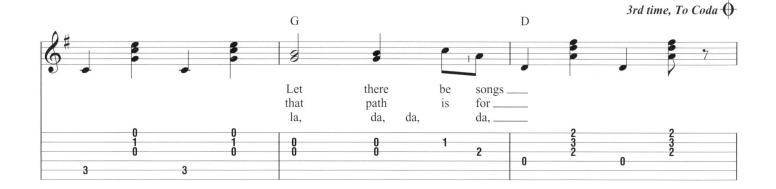

Let there be songs ____
that path is for ____
la, da, da, da, ____

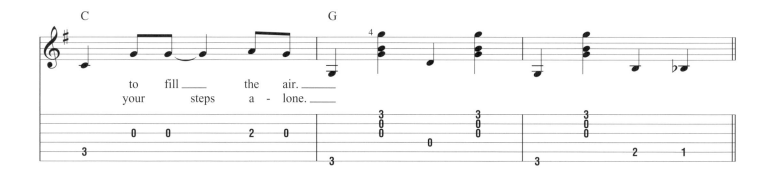

to fill ____ the air. ____
your steps a - lone. ____

Bridge

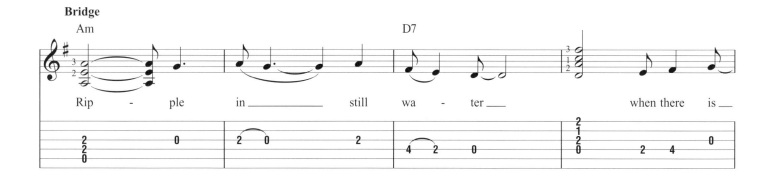

Rip - ple in _____ still wa - ter ____ when there is ____

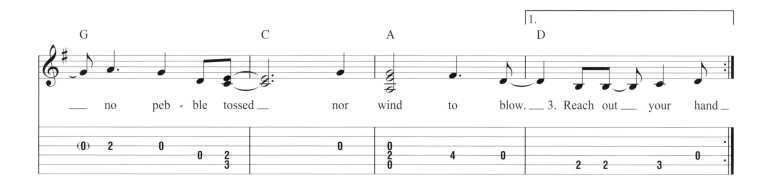

____ no peb - ble tossed ____ nor wind to blow. ____ 3. Reach out ____ your hand ____

1.

2. *D.S. al Coda*

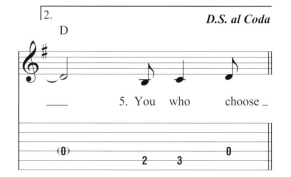

____ 5. You who choose ____

⊕ **Coda**

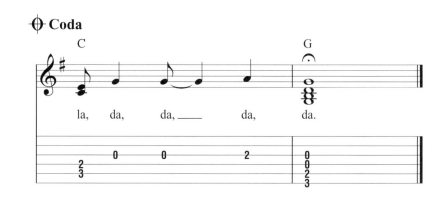

la, da, da, ____ da, da.

This series will help you play your favorite songs quickly and easily. Just follow the tab and listen to the audio to hear how the guitar should sound, and then play along using the separate backing tracks.

Playback tools are provided for slowing down the tempo without changing pitch and looping challenging parts. The melody and lyrics are included in the book so that you can sing or simply follow along.

1. ROCK
00699570.....................$17.99

2. ACOUSTIC
00699569.....................$16.99

3. HARD ROCK
00699573.....................$17.99

4. POP/ROCK
00699571.....................$16.99

5. THREE CHORD SONGS
00300985.....................$16.99

6. '90S ROCK
00298615.....................$16.99

7. BLUES
00699575.....................$19.99

8. ROCK
00699585.....................$16.99

9. EASY ACOUSTIC SONGS
00151708.....................$16.99

10. ACOUSTIC
00699586.....................$16.95

11. EARLY ROCK
00699579.....................$15.99

12. ROCK POP
00291724.....................$16.99

14. BLUES ROCK
00699582.....................$16.99

15. R&B
00699583.....................$17.99

16. JAZZ
00699584.....................$16.99

17. COUNTRY
00699588.....................$17.99

18. ACOUSTIC ROCK
00699577.....................$15.95

20. ROCKABILLY
00699580.....................$17.99

21. SANTANA
00174525.....................$17.99

22. CHRISTMAS
00699600.....................$15.99

23. SURF
00699635.....................$17.99

24. ERIC CLAPTON
00699649.....................$19.99

25. THE BEATLES
00198265.....................$19.99

26. ELVIS PRESLEY
00699643.....................$16.99

27. DAVID LEE ROTH
00699645.....................$16.95

28. GREG KOCH
00699646.....................$19.99

29. BOB SEGER
00699647.....................$16.99

30. KISS
00699644.....................$17.99

32. THE OFFSPRING
00699653.....................$14.95

33. ACOUSTIC CLASSICS
00699656.....................$19.99

34. CLASSIC ROCK
00699658.....................$17.99

35. HAIR METAL
00699660.....................$17.99

36. SOUTHERN ROCK
00699661.....................$19.99

37. ACOUSTIC UNPLUGGED
00699662.....................$22.99

38. BLUES
00699663.....................$17.99

39. '80S METAL
00699664.....................$17.99

40. INCUBUS
00699668.....................$17.95

41. ERIC CLAPTON
00699669.....................$17.99

42. COVER BAND HITS
00211597.....................$16.99

43. LYNYRD SKYNYRD
00699681.....................$22.99

44. JAZZ GREATS
00699689.....................$16.99

45. TV THEMES
00699718.....................$14.95

46. MAINSTREAM ROCK
00699722.....................$16.95

47. HENDRIX SMASH HITS
00699723.....................$19.99

48. AEROSMITH CLASSICS
00699724.....................$17.99

49. STEVIE RAY VAUGHAN
00699725.....................$17.99

50. VAN HALEN 1978-1984
00110269.....................$19.99

51. ALTERNATIVE '90S
00699727.....................$14.99

52. FUNK
00699728.....................$15.99

53. DISCO
00699729.....................$14.99

54. HEAVY METAL
00699730.....................$17.99

55. POP METAL
00699731.....................$14.95

57. GUNS N' ROSES
00159922.....................$17.99

58. BLINK-182
00699772.....................$14.95

59. CHET ATKINS
00702347.....................$17.99

60. 3 DOORS DOWN
00699774.....................$14.95

62. CHRISTMAS CAROLS
00699798.....................$12.95

63. CREEDENCE CLEARWATER REVIVAL
00699802.....................$17.99

64. OZZY OSBOURNE
00699803.....................$19.99

66. THE ROLLING STONES
00699807.....................$19.99

67. BLACK SABBATH
00699808.....................$17.99

68. PINK FLOYD – DARK SIDE OF THE MOON
00699809.....................$17.99

71. CHRISTIAN ROCK
00699824.....................$14.95

72. ACOUSTIC '90S
00699827.....................$14.95

73. BLUESY ROCK
00699829.....................$17.99

74. SIMPLE STRUMMING SONGS
00151706.....................$19.99

75. TOM PETTY
00699882.....................$19.99

76. COUNTRY HITS
00699884.....................$16.99

77. BLUEGRASS
00699910.....................$17.99

78. NIRVANA
00700132.....................$17.99

79. NEIL YOUNG
00700133.....................$24.99

81. ROCK ANTHOLOGY
00700176.....................$22.99

82. EASY ROCK SONGS
00700177.....................$17.99

84. STEELY DAN
00700200.....................$19.99

85. THE POLICE
00700269.....................$16.99

86. BOSTON
00700465.....................$19.99

87. ACOUSTIC WOMEN
00700763.....................$14.99

88. GRUNGE
00700467.....................$16.99

89. REGGAE
00700468.....................$15.99

90. CLASSICAL POP
00700469.....................$14.99

91. BLUES INSTRUMENTALS
00700505.....................$19.99

92. EARLY ROCK INSTRUMENTALS
00700506.....................$17.99

93. ROCK INSTRUMENTALS
00700507.....................$17.99

94. SLOW BLUES
00700508.....................$16.99

95. BLUES CLASSICS
00700509.....................$15.99

96. BEST COUNTRY HITS
00211615.....................$16.99

97. CHRISTMAS CLASSICS
00236542.....................$14.99

98. ROCK BAND
00700704.....................$14.95

99. ZZ TOP
00700762.....................$16.99

100. B.B. KING
00700466.....................$16.99

101. SONGS FOR BEGINNERS
00701917.....................$14.99

102. CLASSIC PUNK
00700769.....................$14.99

104. DUANE ALLMAN
00700846.....................$22.99

105. LATIN
00700939.....................$16.99

106. WEEZER
00700958.....................$17.99

107. CREAM
00701069 .... $17.99

108. THE WHO
00701053 .... $17.99

109. STEVE MILLER
00701054 .... $19.99

110. SLIDE GUITAR HITS
00701055 .... $17.99

111. JOHN MELLENCAMP
00701056 .... $14.99

112. QUEEN
00701052 .... $16.99

113. JIM CROCE
00701058 .... $19.99

114. BON JOVI
00701060 .... $17.99

115. JOHNNY CASH
00701070 .... $17.99

116. THE VENTURES
00701124 .... $17.99

117. BRAD PAISLEY
00701224 .... $16.99

118. ERIC JOHNSON
00701353 .... $17.99

119. AC/DC CLASSICS
00701356 .... $19.99

120. PROGRESSIVE ROCK
00701457 .... $14.99

121. U2
00701508 .... $17.99

122. CROSBY, STILLS & NASH
00701610 .... $16.99

123. LENNON & McCARTNEY ACOUSTIC
00701614 .... $16.99

124. SMOOTH JAZZ
00200664 .... $16.99

125. JEFF BECK
00701687 .... $19.99

126. BOB MARLEY
00701701 .... $17.99

127. 1970S ROCK
00701739 .... $17.99

128. 1960S ROCK
00701740 .... $14.99

129. MEGADETH
00701741 .... $17.99

130. IRON MAIDEN
00701742 .... $17.99

131. 1990S ROCK
00701743 .... $14.99

132. COUNTRY ROCK
00701757 .... $15.99

133. TAYLOR SWIFT
00701894 .... $16.99

135. MINOR BLUES
00151350 .... $17.99

136. GUITAR THEMES
00701922 .... $14.99

137. IRISH TUNES
00701966 .... $15.99

138. BLUEGRASS CLASSICS
00701967 .... $17.99

139. GARY MOORE
00702370 .... $17.99

140. MORE STEVIE RAY VAUGHAN
00702396 .... $19.99

141. ACOUSTIC HITS
00702401 .... $16.99

142. GEORGE HARRISON
00237697 .... $17.99

143. SLASH
00702425 .... $19.99

144. DJANGO REINHARDT
00702531 .... $17.99

145. DEF LEPPARD
00702532 .... $19.99

146. ROBERT JOHNSON
00702533 .... $16.99

147. SIMON & GARFUNKEL
14041591 .... $17.99

148. BOB DYLAN
14041592 .... $17.99

149. AC/DC HITS
14041593 .... $19.99

150. ZAKK WYLDE
02501717 .... $19.99

151. J.S. BACH
02501730 .... $16.99

152. JOE BONAMASSA
02501751 .... $24.99

153. RED HOT CHILI PEPPERS
00702990 .... $22.99

155. ERIC CLAPTON – FROM THE ALBUM UNPLUGGED
00703085 .... $17.99

156. SLAYER
00703770 .... $19.99

157. FLEETWOOD MAC
00101382 .... $17.99

159. WES MONTGOMERY
00102593 .... $22.99

160. T-BONE WALKER
00102641 .... $17.99

161. THE EAGLES – ACOUSTIC
00102659 .... $19.99

162. THE EAGLES HITS
00102667 .... $17.99

163. PANTERA
00103036 .... $19.99

164. VAN HALEN 1986-1995
00110270 .... $19.99

165. GREEN DAY
00210343 .... $17.99

166. MODERN BLUES
00700764 .... $16.99

167. DREAM THEATER
00111938 .... $24.99

168. KISS
00113421 .... $17.99

169. TAYLOR SWIFT
00115982 .... $16.99

170. THREE DAYS GRACE
00117337 .... $16.99

171. JAMES BROWN
00117420 .... $16.99

172. THE DOOBIE BROTHERS
00119670 .... $17.99

173. TRANS-SIBERIAN ORCHESTRA
00119907 .... $19.99

174. SCORPIONS
00122119 .... $19.99

175. MICHAEL SCHENKER
00122127 .... $17.99

176. BLUES BREAKERS WITH JOHN MAYALL & ERIC CLAPTON
00122132 .... $19.99

177. ALBERT KING
00123271 .... $17.99

178. JASON MRAZ
00124165 .... $17.99

179. RAMONES
00127073 .... $16.99

180. BRUNO MARS
00129706 .... $16.99

181. JACK JOHNSON
00129854 .... $16.99

182. SOUNDGARDEN
00138161 .... $17.99

183. BUDDY GUY
00138240 .... $17.99

184. KENNY WAYNE SHEPHERD
00138258 .... $17.99

185. JOE SATRIANI
00139457 .... $19.99

186. GRATEFUL DEAD
00139459 .... $17.99

187. JOHN DENVER
00140839 .... $19.99

188. MÖTLEY CRUE
00141145 .... $19.99

189. JOHN MAYER
00144350 .... $19.99

190. DEEP PURPLE
00146152 .... $19.99

191. PINK FLOYD CLASSICS
00146164 .... $17.99

192. JUDAS PRIEST
00151352 .... $19.99

193. STEVE VAI
00156028 .... $19.99

194. PEARL JAM
00157925 .... $17.99

195. METALLICA: 1983-1988
00234291 .... $22.99

196. METALLICA: 1991-2016
00234292 .... $19.99

HAL•LEONARD®

For complete songlists, visit
Hal Leonard online at
www.halleonard.com

Prices, contents, and availability subject to
change without notice.

EASY GUITAR
WITH NOTES & TAB

This series features simplified arrangements with notes, tab, chord charts, and strum and pick patterns.

MIXED FOLIOS

00702287 Acoustic....$19.99	00196954 Contemporary Disney....$19.99	00702268 1990s Rock....$24.99
00702002 Acoustic Rock Hits for Easy Guitar....$15.99	00702239 Country Classics for Easy Guitar....$24.99	00369043 Rock Songs for Kids....$14.99
00702166 All-Time Best Guitar Collection....$19.99	00702257 Easy Acoustic Guitar Songs....$17.99	00109725 Once....$14.99
00702232 Best Acoustic Songs for Easy Guitar....$16.99	00702041 Favorite Hymns for Easy Guitar....$12.99	00702187 Selections from O Brother Where Art Thou?....$19.99
00119835 Best Children's Songs....$16.99	00222701 Folk Pop Songs....$17.99	00702178 100 Songs for Kids....$16.99
00703055 The Big Book of Nursery Rhymes & Children's Songs....$16.99	00126894 Frozen....$14.99	00702515 Pirates of the Caribbean....$17.99
00698978 Big Christmas Collection....$19.99	00333922 Frozen 2....$14.99	00702125 Praise and Worship for Guitar....$14.99
00702394 Bluegrass Songs for Easy Guitar....$15.99	00702286 Glee....$16.99	00287930 Songs from *A Star Is Born, The Greatest Showman, La La Land,* and More Movie Musicals....$16.99
00289632 Bohemian Rhapsody....$19.99	00702160 The Great American Country Songbook...$19.99	00702285 Southern Rock Hits....$12.99
00703387 Celtic Classics....$16.99	00702148 Great American Gospel for Guitar....$14.99	00156420 Star Wars Music....$16.99
00224808 Chart Hits of 2016-2017....$14.99	00702050 Great Classical Themes for Easy Guitar....$9.99	00121535 30 Easy Celtic Guitar Solos....$16.99
00267383 Chart Hits of 2017-2018....$14.99	00275088 The Greatest Showman....$17.99	00244654 Top Hits of 2017....$14.99
00334293 Chart Hits of 2019-2020....$16.99	00148030 Halloween Guitar Songs....$14.99	00283786 Top Hits of 2018....$14.99
00403479 Chart Hits of 2021-2022....$16.99	00702273 Irish Songs....$14.99	00302269 Top Hits of 2019....$14.99
00702149 Children's Christian Songbook....$9.99	00192503 Jazz Classics for Easy Guitar....$16.99	00355779 Top Hits of 2020....$14.99
00702028 Christmas Classics....$8.99	00702275 Jazz Favorites for Easy Guitar....$17.99	00374083 Top Hits of 2021....$16.99
00101779 Christmas Guitar....$14.99	00702274 Jazz Standards for Easy Guitar....$19.99	00702294 Top Worship Hits....$17.99
00702141 Classic Rock....$8.95	00702162 Jumbo Easy Guitar Songbook....$24.99	00702255 VH1's 100 Greatest Hard Rock Songs....$34.99
00159642 Classical Melodies....$12.99	00232285 La La Land....$16.99	00702175 VH1's 100 Greatest Songs of Rock and Roll....$34.99
00253933 Disney/Pixar's Coco....$16.99	00702258 Legends of Rock....$14.99	00702253 Wicked....$12.99
00702203 CMT's 100 Greatest Country Songs....$34.99	00702189 MTV's 100 Greatest Pop Songs....$34.99	
00702283 The Contemporary Christian Collection....$16.99	00702272 1950s Rock....$16.99	
	00702271 1960s Rock....$16.99	
	00702270 1970s Rock....$24.99	
	00702269 1980s Rock....$16.99	

ARTIST COLLECTIONS

00702267 AC/DC for Easy Guitar....$16.99	00702245 Elton John — Greatest Hits 1970–2002....$19.99	00702252 Frank Sinatra — Nothing But the Best....$12.99
00156221 Adele – 25....$16.99	00129855 Jack Johnson....$17.99	00702010 Best of Rod Stewart....$17.99
00396889 Adele – 30....$19.99	00702204 Robert Johnson....$16.99	00702049 Best of George Strait....$17.99
00702040 Best of the Allman Brothers....$16.99	00702234 Selections from Toby Keith — 35 Biggest Hits....$12.95	00702259 Taylor Swift for Easy Guitar....$15.99
00702865 J.S. Bach for Easy Guitar....$15.99	00702003 Kiss....$16.99	00359800 Taylor Swift – Easy Guitar Anthology....$24.99
00702169 Best of The Beach Boys....$16.99	00702216 Lynyrd Skynyrd....$17.99	00702260 Taylor Swift — Fearless....$14.99
00702292 The Beatles — 1....$22.99	00702182 The Essential Bob Marley....$16.99	00139727 Taylor Swift — 1989....$19.99
00125796 Best of Chuck Berry....$16.99	00146081 Maroon 5....$14.99	00115960 Taylor Swift — Red....$16.99
00702201 The Essential Black Sabbath....$15.99	00121925 Bruno Mars – Unorthodox Jukebox....$12.99	00253667 Taylor Swift — Reputation....$17.99
00702250 blink-182 — Greatest Hits....$17.99	00702248 Paul McCartney — All the Best....$14.99	00702290 Taylor Swift — Speak Now....$16.99
02501615 Zac Brown Band — The Foundation....$17.99	00125484 The Best of MercyMe....$12.99	00232849 Chris Tomlin Collection – 2nd Edition....$14.99
02501621 Zac Brown Band — You Get What You Give....$16.99	00702209 Steve Miller Band — Young Hearts (Greatest Hits)....$12.95	00702226 Chris Tomlin — See the Morning....$12.95
00702043 Best of Johnny Cash....$17.99	00124167 Jason Mraz....$15.99	00148643 Train....$14.99
00702090 Eric Clapton's Best....$16.99	00702096 Best of Nirvana....$16.99	00702427 U2 — 18 Singles....$19.99
00702086 Eric Clapton — from the Album Unplugged....$17.99	00702211 The Offspring — Greatest Hits....$17.99	00702108 Best of Stevie Ray Vaughan....$17.99
00702202 The Essential Eric Clapton....$17.99	00138026 One Direction....$17.99	00279005 The Who....$14.99
00702053 Best of Patsy Cline....$17.99	00702030 Best of Roy Orbison....$17.99	00702123 Best of Hank Williams....$15.99
00222697 Very Best of Coldplay – 2nd Edition....$17.99	00702144 Best of Ozzy Osbourne....$14.99	00194548 Best of John Williams....$14.99
00702229 The Very Best of Creedence Clearwater Revival....$16.99	00702279 Tom Petty....$17.99	00702228 Neil Young — Greatest Hits....$17.99
00702145 Best of Jim Croce....$16.99	00102911 Pink Floyd....$17.99	00119133 Neil Young — Harvest....$14.99
00702278 Crosby, Stills & Nash....$12.99	00702139 Elvis Country Favorites....$19.99	
14042809 Bob Dylan....$15.99	00702293 The Very Best of Prince....$19.99	
00702276 Fleetwood Mac — Easy Guitar Collection....$17.99	00699415 Best of Queen for Guitar....$16.99	
00139462 The Very Best of Grateful Dead....$16.99	00109279 Best of R.E.M.....$14.99	
00702136 Best of Merle Haggard....$16.99	00702208 Red Hot Chili Peppers — Greatest Hits....$17.99	
00702227 Jimi Hendrix — Smash Hits....$19.99	00198960 The Rolling Stones....$17.99	
00702288 Best of Hillsong United....$12.99	00174793 The Very Best of Santana....$16.99	
00702236 Best of Antonio Carlos Jobim....$15.99	00702196 Best of Bob Seger....$16.99	
	00146046 Ed Sheeran....$17.99	

Prices, contents and availability subject to change without notice.

Visit Hal Leonard online at **halleonard.com**